LIVING IN A REAL-TIME WORLD

6 Capabilities to Prepare Us
for an Unimaginable Future

Jim Selman

www.real-timeworld.com

ISBN 9781796461138

CREDITS

Cover design and print layout by Patrick Broom
www.patrickbroom.com

Editing by Shae Hadden
www.shaehadden.com

Author headshot by Carl Studna
www.carlstudna.com

DEDICATION

*To the Young, who show us what's possible,
and the Old, who give us wisdom and
meaning...if we are listening.*

CONTENTS

PREFACE

"We cannot put off living until we are ready. The most salient characteristic of life is its urgency, 'here and now' without any possible postponement. Life is fired at us point blank."

José Ortega y Gasset[1]

We live in perplexing times.

Until sometime right around now, we could afford to wait and see which way things were going before committing to a certain course of action. We could "get ready, get set and go". But we no longer have the luxury of time to prepare before the next thing is fired at us. We no longer have the luxury of waiting for things to unfold. We operate in real time, that perpetually urgent present that has us proceeding straight to "go". We used to look years ahead, now it's months and weeks. Even the idea of living one *day* at a time is shifting to living one *moment* at a time.

The idea of living in the present moment—not in the past or the future—is relatively easy to understand. But it's not so easy to do. Constantly living in the present is living life as a meditation, embracing every moment as an original. Constantly living in the present is recognizing that everything is action and acknowledging that many of the choices we are facing and many of the actions we are taking are originals too.

That is because, whether we like it or not, our world is changing at an exponential pace. Many areas of our civilization are converging and putting increasing pressure on the planetary systems on which all life depends. How will conditions on Earth be affected? No one can say with certainty.

Two further questions arise. Can we change our worldview to deal with these new and unpredictable realities? And can we be ready to navigate and respond to the changes that will happen in our lifetime and in our children's lifetime?

I believe we can.

Although this little book includes some nuggets of wisdom garnered from my many years as a transformational leader, consultant and coach, my objective is not to tell you how to be a better leader or a better human being. These insights and reflections are about the personal and professional challenges of all people today. I offer no solutions, no answers. No techniques or handy tips. My intention is to reveal a kind of cognitive blindness we all share and to provoke you, the reader, to challenge your basic assumptions about the world and about life.

I don't believe we face insurmountable technical problems. I believe that, on a deeper level, we have some profound philosophical blind spots and tough questions with which we can engage. Questions that, if ignored, will undoubtedly result in the persistence of the most pressing problems we are seeking to solve. Questions such as:

Can we accelerate our own evolution?

What new ways of being and observing the world will enable us to live in the present while simultaneously maintaining coherence within a larger context, purpose, or longer term intention?

Is it possible to produce a step change in how we learn?

In a world of permanent uncertainty and accelerating change, what competencies and skills will we require? What approach to learning and education will work in a real-time world?

Can we change our relationship to the world and life in such a way that we have less stress, anxiety, and resignation?

Is there a way to master or "tune" the way we experience the world, our past, our present, and our future? Is it possible to live in a positive relationship with constant uncertainty, exponential change, and our own mortality?

These kinds of questions may never be answered definitively, but we live our answers every day.

I believe we can design our own reality and perhaps the future of mankind. We can create a new narrative of what it means to be a human being. I would hope that, as we do so, we can retain what has made us uniquely human in the past—love, compassion, generosity, joy, creativity, and wonder—and that we can maintain our connection with the human spirit.

That is why I wrote this book. The scale and scope of change today challenges each of us. I see many people wrestling with the question of what to do with the rest of their life in the midst of a perpetually changing reality. Even more people are feeling lost and disoriented and struggling to cope. It's as if we have all suddenly been given the job of "adventurer" and we all need to navigate our way through a dynamic and ever-evolving world.

- What will help us get oriented?
- What should we pay attention to?
- What can we let go of?
- What abilities can we cultivate to navigate more effectively?

These are some of the questions I've been living with for the last while. I've spent my life working on questions of how human beings can, individually and in groups, realize the possibility of accomplishing breakthroughs at scale *no matter what the circumstances.* Considering the urgency of the world's problems and the fact that we are always navigating through life, you may find some of these reflections to be useful.

I don't know where the world is headed. Much of it isn't working; much of it is being disrupted. At the same time, we're seeing new technologies and possibilities emerging faster than most of us can comprehend. I don't believe *anyone* has any idea where we are all going. So if you're looking for predictions about the future in this book, you'll be disappointed.

But if you're wanting to know what you can do right now to better prepare yourself for navigating through an unknown future, you won't be disappointed. And you won't be disappointed if you're looking to explore how life can be satisfying and meaningful and what capabilities we already have that we can cultivate to live well in an emerging world where we don't know exactly where we're headed or how we will get there.

Navigating successfully doesn't depend on knowing where we're going. Navigating successfully in a real-time world is not a matter of orienting ourselves to a specific destination which, while we can speculate, we can't really know. It is a matter of orienting ourselves to where we came from and where we are—which we *do* know.

So where did we come from? Where are we? These are ultimately existential questions because we can't separate *where* we are from *who* we are. We are all products of history. Not just in the geographical sense of location, but also in the existential sense of our purpose and relationships, our traditions and practices, our worldview and our values.

Like Leif Erikson, the first known European to navigate the Atlantic and discover continental North America, we can set out from wherever we are now, knowing what we believe, knowing the culture and the land in which we grew up. We will inevitably encounter the unexpected, get blown off course, make landfall in unanticipated places. As we navigate our way through what's emerging in front of us, we will begin to perceive ourselves, others, and our circumstances differently.

You may feel called to share what you discover through reading this book with others as a conversation starter. I invite you to do so. In terms of knowing where we are, nothing is fixed, permanent, or assured. What *is* assured is that we will evolve, just as this conversation will evolve. My hope is that as many people as possible become responsible navigators, comfortable moving through a dynamic reality without maps, living each moment as an original, responding with ease to the changes in the world.

What follows are some basic ideas to help you orient yourself. It's entirely up to each of us where, when, and how we navigate through our lives and in the worlds we create.

Jim Selman
September 2018
Ojai, CA

ACKNOWLEDGMENTS

This manuscript would not exist without the commitment, professionalism and support of Shae Hadden. She has been my coach, editor, architect, and friend from the beginning of this project. Like all good coaches, she has kept me focused and inspired with the possibility of what we were creating, while being unreasonable and determined that I keep to my deadlines and not succumb to the endless distractions so prevalent in this real-time world.

I have been a student and friend of Dr. Fernando Flores for almost 40 years. Fernando has shown me that commitment, one of the core themes of this book, is action in language and the basis for co-creation and coordination. Over the years, his work has encompassed the entire spectrum of human experience and offered us an ongoing ontological inquiry into the nature of human beings and our relationship to the world. His philosophical work on the nature of 'being', moods, possibilities, and trust have inspired and awakened me to the limits of my own thinking, as well as to the power of language and conversation to free us from our traditional worldviews.

I want to thank my friend Gay Hendricks for his mentorship in my undertaking any writing effort. His feedback has helped me rethink how I communicate and relate with my audience and sets a standard of excellence that I continue to aspire to. I want to also thank Rick Fullerton, Robert Orr, Ron Donovan, and Liv Wright for their willingness to read the manuscript in the rough and give us the kind of candid feedback that has hopefully resulted in this being more useful and relevant to all of my readers.

Finally, I want to thank my wife Darlene Patrick for her love and confidence in me and for always being available as a rigorous thought partner when I would become lost, confused, or discouraged on the journey.

Chapter 1

REAL TIME

*"While the magnitude of the coming change doesn't
bother me, it is the speed of the change
I'm worried about."*

Peter Diamandis,
Co-founder & Chairman of Singularity University[1]

The days of "slow" change are over.

We are now living in what I call a "real-time world", a world in which we can no longer trust our past to inform us about what will happen in the future. A world in which what's emerging is also constantly forcing us to revise and change our stories about how the world works.

The most compelling aspects of life today are accelerating change, increasing complexity, unpredictability, and uncertainty. The scope, scale, and speed with which our new reality is unfolding is beyond anything we've ever faced. We used to say, "The more things change, the more they stay the same." Today, it is more accurate to say that the more things change, the faster everything changes.

We're bombarded daily with a dizzying array of disruption from around the world—everything geopolitical upheavals and technological advances to environmental disasters and social unrest. Many of us are talking about these large-scale changes because we know they affect us all. Many of us are trying to make sense of what's happening, trying to understand why it's happening and what this might mean for our future.

Some say we're in the midst of a revolution and that the old systems are being overthrown. Others say it is evolution, part of a gradual development into a more complex form of life. Whether it's evolution or revolution isn't an issue that will be decided right now. History will determine which it is and whether the changes we are experiencing are beneficial or detrimental.

I believe we are in the midst of a global transformation, a planetary-wide paradigm shift in which we are changing ourselves and our relationship to our reality.

A paradigm is a mental model, a worldview, a set of ideas that frames how we observe reality. It is how reality "shows up" for us and, most importantly, it informs how we navigate in life. Within a given paradigm, we don't have a choice about *what* shows up, but we always have a choice about *how we relate* to what is showing up.

When what's happening no longer conforms to our paradigm, our traditional worldview (that historical understanding of who we are, our relationships with everyone and everything, and our understanding of life itself) breaks down. Most, if not all, of the major, seemingly intractable problems and technological breakthroughs we hear about today are the consequence of this kind of breakdown. What was familiar "common sense" no longer makes sense when the world is no longer "familiar" or common.

Along with the widely recognized threats we now face from climate change and declining resources, we are observing increasingly widespread clashes of ideologies, cultures, and values. When combined with instant communications and global connectivity, these issues touch every aspect of our lives in every part of the world.

Humanity has been through paradigm shifts before. I believe that, in general, most of the changes that have occurred are moving us in a more positive direction. However, what makes this particular transformation problematic is its speed: it seems to be happening almost faster than we have the capacity to comprehend. Not only is the speed of change personally disorienting and systemically disruptive. It's also altering our relationship to time. This transformation is not *inherently* bad or *inherently* good.

It's just very uncomfortable while we're in the middle of it.

Propositions

When I began my career in the 1960s, computers were information machines for sorting and reporting data. As processing speeds got faster and faster, the gap in time between inputs and outputs became smaller and smaller. At some point, the gap, for all practical purposes, disappeared and machines began to operate in "real time". Computers changed from being information and reporting machines to being integral components of systems performing a wide variety of tasks, such as controlling industrial processes, on time, every time. The robotic and AI explosion we're witnessing today are extensions of this capability.

Today the accelerating rate of change means the gap between our past and our future is becoming smaller and smaller—exactly when many forces are converging in our history. The consequence of this gap disappearing is that we no longer have the time to deal with problems like we used to. As these forces converge, we are realizing we have choices to make, choices that would have been unimaginable in the not-too-distant past and which will determine the future of life on Earth.

There are many practices from meditation to extreme sports that help people become more conscious and skilled at living moment to moment. Most traditions about how to live in the present tend to be an aspect of spiritual or metaphysical practices. Many of these "paths" suggest that learning to be present is a choice an individual has and that their practices, once mastered, can assure serenity and well-being.

Indeed, throughout history, many writers and teachers have pointed to the fact that everything that is happening is always and only happening in the present moment. For instance, Eckhart Tolle's best-selling book *The Power of Now*, a recent addition to this literature, takes readers on a spiritual journey to give us an understanding of what a difference it can make to our experience of living when we connect with this fundamental fact of our existence.[2] The world is "there" and our choice is to learn how to "be here now"—to be in touch with our bodies and experience without being prisoners of our thinking and internal conversations. While I agree with most of these teachings about the value of living in the "now", they all tend to focus on the individual's experience in the context of a more or less stable world or a world that changes slowly over long periods of time. In the context of slow change, a person can be unaware or ignorant of the "power of now" and still be able to connect with what is going on and plan for the future, participate and function in the world, even achieve success.

Our "world" today is no longer changing slowly over time. We live in a dynamic real-time world in which living in the present is no longer a choice reserved for those who wish to pursue a particular spiritual path or lifestyle. Whether we like it or not, we are all learning how to navigate this paradigm and coordinate with others—learning how to live our lives, survive, and not become obsolete—in real time.

The implications of this can trap us in a mood of fear and powerlessness. Or they can be a catalyst for unprecedented ambition and creativity. We can, like deer caught in headlights, freeze and watch our own destruction. Or we can, if we effectively figure out how to navigate in real time, move forward and literally create our future as we go.

We are just beginning to confront what is required of us as we move forward into a world of permanent uncertainty and accelerating change. We are realizing we have less and less control over what is emerging at any level—global, institutional, organizational, community, or personal. Many millions of us feel overwhelmed. Many, resigned or cynical, believe that our situation is so hopeless that any positive or optimistic scenario is either naiveté or sheer fantasy. Others (myself included) are engaged in reinventing their understanding of the world and cultivating inherent capabilities and positive moods to navigate and succeed in this emerging reality.

Our exploration of how to navigate in real time begins with the following propositions and observations.

1. We have never been here before.

No one has 100% certainty about what is happening, let alone can tell us what we should do with total confidence. No one knows the future. No one knows where we are going. We can no longer trust our past, including much of our knowledge and common sense, to guide our decisions. This doesn't mean our past or our common sense are irrelevant: it means they are simply information and not frameworks for decision-making.

2. We need more critical thinking.

Critical thinking is not about getting to the right answer. It is about creating openings and having choices. In a world we can't control, this is essential. When we learn to think critically, we can see some of the limitations and blind spots in our habitual ways of thinking. For example, viewing what's happening through the lens of "either/or" thinking (that is, either the individual *or* the group, either short *or* long-term, either right *or* wrong, either true *or* false) leaves us with a very limited set of black-and-white options and a bundle of dilemmas. Viewing it through the lens of "both/and" thinking can give us access to dynamic possibilities that disappear dilemmas and cultivate moods conducive to creativity and innovation.

3. We are challenging all assumptions.

Technology is forcing us to revisit our most basic assumptions about everything—from politics to science, jobs to relationships. For example, one of our most basic assumptions is that the source of leadership is the individual, usually someone endowed with special capabilities, vision, or charisma. We can challenge this assumption and look at leadership as a social phenomenon, since leadership doesn't make any sense without at least two people. This notion of leadership in a social context can be seen even more clearly when we consider that, while individuals make commitments, we always need others to fulfill our commitments. In challenging this and many other assumptions, we can become different observers and appreciate that, in most instances, we are co-creating our future in every moment.

4. We always have a choice in how we *relate*.

How we relate to the world influences how well we navigate a perpetually changing reality and what we can create together. When we don't have maps and no one knows where we're going, five key relationships help us get oriented: our relationship with ourselves, each other, our circumstances, time, and whatever is beyond our understanding. To choose a relationship with something, like any choice, is a commitment. A commitment is an action in language, which is why conversations are so central to how we create the future.

5. We live in conversations.

Whatever our understanding of reality is, it is always an interpretation. Whether we are in a dialogue or a discussion, listening to self-talk, or even just thinking, we are creating and interpreting reality in all our conversations. Every conversation has consequences— even if nothing happens, which is also an outcome. Before the era of real time (and even today), most of our conversations were from the perspective of a spectator: they were conversations about change, about what's happening and why. Few of these discussions, com- mentaries, opinions, and points of view make much difference in the present. Spectators don't normally affect action. In the era of real time, people who are having great impact are doing so by engaging a different set of conversational capabilities, such as distinguishing the difference between explanations for change and conversations that change something. These capabilities are inherent to all humans and we can develop and use them to collectively produce the future we want.

6. We are co-creating the future.

Communication and relationship can be seen as heads and tails of the same coin. It's difficult to imagine communicating in the absence of a relationship and equally difficult to imagine having a relationship without communication. Both are basic to co-creating reality. The world of today is a product of what has come before us in this regard: it is the outcome of all the relationships and all the conversations of everyone who has ever lived up to this point in time. Likewise, the future—the world of tomorrow—will be a product of our relationships and our conversations today.

7. We are all leaders and navigators.

We are living in a world of accelerating change, increasing complexity, and escalating unpredictability. We are entering new territories in many domains of life, territories for which we have no maps. Without maps, no one knows what destinations even exist, let alone how to get to them. It is as if we are explorers in a "Star Trek" universe, going, as they say, "where no one has gone before". Traveling through life in this way, we look to our leaders (and we are all leaders on this journey) to be our navigators, to orient us to where we are in the present and what is possible, given where we have come from and what is happening now. Without skilled navigators, we are literally lost in an ocean of change.

Getting Oriented

The Internet has made it possible for us to see more of what's happening in our world than at any previous time in history. We can only marginally begin to understand the scope and scale of what we are observing. Everything is moving so fast that what we learn is often obsolete before we can fully comprehend it. We definitely cannot control what's happening. And we cannot trust our predictions about what will happen next.

Some of us feel as if we are already lost.

Our habitual response to this feeling? Try to anchor ourselves in certainty—as absolute as possible—before we have to choose where we're going next or what we're doing.

In the past, all we needed to orient ourselves was a firm conviction about *something.* Then we could anchor ourselves around *that certainty*, choose a direction and see how to move forward with some confidence. When we're looking for certainty to orient ourselves, we can never get enough information to satisfy us. The future is constantly emerging, constantly being shaped by unpredictable circumstances and unknown contingencies. The search for certainty can become a vicious cycle in which the more assurances we want about the future, the less sure we become. This partly explains why we, as individuals and organizations, tend to hold on tight to what we are certain about, like our belief systems and success formulas. Cast away these anchors and we easily become disoriented.

If we accept the idea that nothing—or next to nothing—is certain in today's real-time world, then what can we use to orient ourselves?

Clarity.

Clarity is different from certainty.

Certainty is a point of view, never a fact. It is a position that—without a doubt—something is or will be true. Certainty attempts to be resolved based on whatever is happening in our external circumstances. Certainty tries to get clear about "the way it is". It tries to answer the question, "What will happen?" When we're looking for certainty, we search outside ourselves for more information—and there's never enough. This invites a right/wrong dynamic in which we take sides and defend a particular interest, opinion, or ideology. The belief that anything is certain can leave us polarized and divided. Conversation quickly devolves into arguments about whose belief is right and whose is wrong.

Clarity, on the other hand, is not a point of view. It is a commitment and willingness to see things as they are. Clarity is grounded in the responsibility of the observer. Clarity is about how we see it, and how what we see connects to our concerns. Clarity invites the questions, "What do we want to happen?" and "What are we committed to?" These very questions act as our guidance system and prompt us to come together and build relationships with others so that we can confront perplexing times and thrive. When something's not clear, we can have the conversations and take the actions necessary to clear things up. Orienting ourselves around clarity, when combined with accepting the realities of our real-time world and getting clear about our commitments, makes it possible for us to co-create a future that works for everyone.

Real-Time World

In a real-time world, our choices are not dependent on knowledge. That's not to say knowledge is irrelevant or that critical thinking skills are unnecessary. But when we have to make choices for the long-term future in the midst of high uncertainty, knowledge is neither central nor necessary to effectively functioning and sustaining success. It can often be counter-productive. As comedian Will Rogers observed, "The trouble with most people is not that they don't know much, but that they know so much that isn't true."[3]

In a real-time world, the realization that we have no real and sustainable control over people and circumstances opens a whole world of possibilities previously not available to us. It offers us a new kind of freedom and power, since it leaves us no choice but to accept things as they are. It eliminates the persistence of living in a "would be", "could be", and "should be" relationship with the world. Everything is just what it is. By accepting this fact, we become open to a fundamentally different relationship with the future and can observe new possibilities and choices that weren't previously evident.

We don't need to persist in the illusion that we are going to fix reality. We can begin to create a new one.

In a real-time world, who we are is not permanent or "fixed", but a constantly evolving narrative. This contrasts with the traditional, more stable worldview in which human beings are objects and rarely change in fundamental ways. In a real-time world, we are also always part of the larger whole. We are never separate from or independent of what is occurring: we are always connected to and a part of it. Further, our points of view and even our thinking and moods are not entirely personal or unique to us as individuals. This means we need to reinvent what it means to be "me" and appreciate ourselves as more than just individual actors.

In a real-time world, our ambition is less about goals and fixed plans than about purpose, commitments, and possibility. Possibility can be viewed as the space we work in, the boundaries and scope of our undertaking. Purpose can be seen as our direction; commitments as our actions. These constitute the basis for a kind of guidance system that allows us to navigate whatever is occurring. Just as players in a fast-moving game are always present to different possibilities and organizing themselves to move and respond to what is happening, leaders as navigators are constantly moving in the context of their purpose and commitments. Anything that is inconsistent with purpose and commitments becomes an opportunity for new action. Constraints become the raw material for co-creation.

In a real-time world, the concept of scarcity naturally disappears. Much of our historical commonsense relationship to reality has been based on the idea that there is "not enough" of whatever we want. As a consequence, we have been living in a state of scarcity or insufficiency, always one or more steps behind where we think we need to be in order to have enough. In a real-time world, rather than attempt to acquire more of what we don't have, we accept that at any given moment in time we only have what we have and are, therefore, always sufficient in the moment. When we can embrace the concept of sufficiency, our only choice is to accept the way things are and to create what is missing.

In a real-time world, collaboration and co-creation are fundamentally a constant. Our culture's bias toward identifying the individual actor as the source of results has largely obscured that this has always been the case. Most of the leadership and self-help literature to date has generally attributed results to the actions or attributes of an individual. On examination, we can see that individuals can accomplish virtually none of their individual commitments without other people.

Navigating Now

To navigate successfully in a real-time world, we will need to be fully present in life and co-creating it consciously with others. We may very well need to **trust** people we may not know or perhaps don't understand, **collaborate** with those with whom we may compete, and **coordinate** with those with whom we may disagree. We've always valued and recognized the importance of these three things. In a real-time world, they become essential. Therefore, we will need to be masterful at listening and engaging in committed conversations.

I believe all human beings have, to one degree or another, the conversational capabilities we need. We are all born with these capabilities: they come with being human. However, like any abilities, we are blind to them until we see they are missing. For instance, if you don't know you have an ability to read, it won't occur to you as something you are missing. It is only when someone points out to you that you could read and you see the possibility of being literate for yourself, that you realize that it was missing and begin to learn and cultivate what was already an innate capability.

I've identified six conversational capabilities to focus on in this book, from among many that will be essential for succeeding in real time. In a relatively stable world, we would think of these six as individual attributes, assume that we either have them or we don't, and learn to navigate with whatever we've grown to accept as "the way we are". Most of us don't even notice these as innate capabilities that we can cultivate and develop. In today's relatively unstable world, however, we find ourselves dealing, more and more, with concerns and problems that cannot be solved by working in ways that were successful in the past. I propose that we now need to intentionally cultivate previously unrecognized or underdeveloped capabilities if we are to become effective navigators and leaders.

Each of the following chapters of this book focuses on one capability, expressed as verbs, since we can be continuously cultivating these capabilities in conversations that flow into the "now". And since they are all avenues of our self-expression, each is also referred to as an art.

No matter what we want, who we're with, or where we want to go, these capabilities can help us put the past in the past, let go of attachments to our experience and beliefs, and step into the slipstream of the perpetual present. More importantly, these capabilities can prepare us to embrace the new realities that are continuously emerging and can help us confidently make choices in real time.

The Six Capabilities

1. ACCEPTING: the art of surrender

2. BEING: the art of context

3. LISTENING: the art of mastering moods

4. COMMUNICATING: the art of relating

5. APPROPRIATING: the art of situational learning

6. CARING: the art of love

All six abilities are inter-related. Your effectiveness in one will influence your effectiveness in others. For example, listening, which includes observing your own moods and the moods of others, will affect your capability to relate. And your effectiveness at accepting will impact with whom, what, and how you relate.

For these to be effective navigational aids, we need to recover and develop our capacity for commitment and for living as our word. Nurtured and used together with integrity, these six capabilities can move us closer to gracefully embracing the paradox between living without control and generating new actions and accomplishments.

We don't know where humanity is headed or how things will turn out. But we each have a choice about how we participate here and now.

We can choose to participate by being antagonists of change. We can choose to be spectators to those who are navigating and actively pursuing breakthroughs. Or we can choose to bring a focused and caring presence to our learning and to our participation in global transformation and have some influence in how our personal future, our childrens' future, and the future of our organizations, communities, and planet unfolds.

Life is, indeed, fired at us point blank.

Chapter 2

ACCEPTING:
the art of surrender

*Acceptance is a matter of being rigorously honest
with ourselves that, ultimately, reality doesn't care
what we think.*

Why Surrender?

We've all played with reality.

As children, we imagined ourselves being different people in different roles, living in different times and situations, exploring different planets and solar systems. When we were playing these games, our imaginary worlds were real for us. When we got tired of the reality we were in, we simply shifted the game to a new one. This capability to imagine one reality, commit to it, engage with it and, at some moment, let it go and move on to a different one is inherent in each of us.

Unfortunately, unlike Peter Pan, we don't remain children forever. We have to leave Neverland, the world of ever-changing games where no one ever ages, and grow up. And in growing up, we buy into our culture's prevailing story about "the way it *really* is".

Having one objective reality is practical for adults living in a more or less stable world. When change happens slowly over long periods of time, our common sense can guide us through life. But when things start changing fast in a short period of time, our common sense may make no sense at all. Our different interpretations of reality and our thinking may, in fact, make us anxious, frustrated, resigned and, in some cases, isolated. We can't relate and we feel out of touch. We can start to feel disconnected from each other and from the games we've created in our one "fixed" reality.

Navigating life in real time begins with acknowledging that we really only have one choice in how we relate to anything. We can choose to resist or we can choose to accept "the way it is". It doesn't matter whether we are looking at who we are and how we relate to what is happening around us and other people, how we relate to our own thinking and time, or how we relate to the media and whatever is beyond our comprehension (call it God, the universe, or the mystery of life). The choice always comes down to resist or accept.

In our Western culture, the prevailing paradigm predisposes us to **resist** and to try to control reality. We spend inordinate amounts of time and energy trying to learn "the way it *really* is" and then arguing and defending our points of view on virtually every aspect of reality. Some of us, tired of arguing, opt out and walk away with our point of view intact. Opting out gives us some feeling of control when we're feeling overwhelmed or overpowered.

In a real-time world, "the way it is" is never a fact.

Reality is *always* changing and it's *always* different for different people, depending upon their concerns and commitments, their values, and their historical perspective. It is always an interpretation. Our reality correlates with how we observe the world; change how we observe (our worldview) and we change our world.

Inevitably, doubt will also be an aspect of any relationship, any situation, or any circumstance. If we want to fully participate in life and consciously create together, we will want to get comfortable with both doubt and uncertainty. Because, no matter what relationships, situations, or circumstances we find ourselves in, they will both be there with us.

Getting to absolute certainty about reality is just not possible.

While there are many ways to resist, profound acceptance is straightforward and absolute. It involves being rigorously honest with ourselves, acknowledging that we have no control over reality, and then choosing to let life be exactly the way it is, whether we like it or not and regardless of our point of view. Learning to accept life on life's terms is essentially an act of surrender, an act that alters our relationship with everything.

Developing the capability of accepting is essential if we are to learn how to let go of our ideas and stories of "the way it was" and be open to embracing new contingencies and new realities as they are continually emerging around us. As we master the art of surrender, we can become different observers of what's happening, we can listen to our embodied wisdom, we can distinguish and work with moods. We can have different kinds of conversations in which we are more authentic, creative, and empowered. Previously unimagined possibilities show up. And we can, once again, create new "games" to play together.

Game Over

In today's real-time world, rapid change and increasing complexity are defusing the power of prediction and control. The stories, the rules, and the systems that have governed our reality in the past are breaking down. When we stop resisting and accept that our "old game" is over, when we surrender to what is happening, we take the first step toward creating a new reality.

Surrender is a choice.

Surrender is not succumbing or giving up. Succumbing is being beaten down by circumstances or the opposition until you have to give up or die. It is a "no choice" state of affairs where you lose the game—a state of affairs where you also lose your dignity and the power or possibility of continuing to play. Succumbing leaves you with nothing but resentment and resignation.

Surrender is profound acceptance. It is a choice to profoundly accept circumstances as they are and to declare game over. In the moment of surrender, you are clear that there is no possibility for accomplishing your purpose the way that the game is currently constructed. In the moment of surrender, you retain your dignity and you recover your *self*. When we take responsibility for who we are, we then become the source of how we navigate in life as well as how we show up for other people.

Surrender is acknowledging our responsibility for the choices we make, including choosing to surrender when we can no longer imagine any other possibility. Paradoxically, when we surrender, new possibilities appear.

When we surrender, we can redesign the game we are playing or start a new one.

Giving Up

"Never give up."

That is what most of us were taught to believe. We were instructed to stay the course. Stubbornly hold our resolve. Win at any cost.

There is some value in the notion that if we only try a little harder or be patient long enough that the situation will work itself out and that we will—somehow—achieve our objective. Most progress has come from people's willingness to overcome long odds, to be unreasonably committed, and to take on extraordinary challenges.

And, at the same time, there is a big difference between resisting and denying the way things are and having the resolve to accomplish something that neither you nor anyone else has ever accomplished before. The difference has to do with what endgame we are playing and whether there is still a possibility of winning.

Basketball coach Red Auerbach was famous for always carrying an unlit cigar in his hand during games. At some moment, he would put the cigar into his mouth, clamp down on it, and put his hands on his hips. He told me that this was the moment when *he* decided the game was either won or lost, regardless of the score or how much time was left on the clock. This was a powerful declaration of his commitment to the team's endgame: in this moment, he would surrender to the inevitability of the current game and begin to play the next one.

This first step towards creating a new reality is not rolling over when we encounter obstacles or adversity. It is using whatever we encounter to accomplish what we want. Like sailors navigating a stormy, disrupted ocean, we can use the challenges of tides, the weather, and the various obstacles we meet to navigate where we want to go in life.

Commitment

Surrendering does not mean we are less committed.

Acceptance, after all, is an absolute commitment.

In the moment of surrender, there is no turning back. We accept what's happening and allow ourselves to go with the flow of life. We commit to something larger than ourselves.

In the words of Scottish mountaineer and writer William Hutchison Murray:

"Until one is committed there is hesitancy, the chance to draw back, always ineffectiveness. Concerning all acts of initiative (and creation), there is one elementary truth, the ignorance of which kills countless ideas and splendid plans: that the moment one definitely commits oneself, then Providence moves too. All sorts of things occur to help one that would never otherwise have occurred. A whole stream of events issues from the decision, raising in one's favor all manner of unforeseen incidents and meetings and material assistance, which no man could have dreamt would have come his way."[1]

When we commit absolutely, three things happen:

1. We transform our relationship to everything.
2. We become different observers.
3. We open ourselves to possibilities that were not previously available to us or that did not even exist before.

Anyone trapped in a heavily habitual, counter-productive behavior, for example, makes an absolute commitment when they surrender to the fact that they have no control over the behavior and cannot manage by themselves. They essentially commit to "no possibility of control".

This naturally changes their relationship to their central issue. If there is no possibility, then the only option is to create a possibility where none exists—and that will require the participation of others, since the individual has demonstrated and now committed to the fact that they cannot "do it alone". As this new and previously unavailable possibility unfolds, myriad other possibilities appear as well: new relationships, employment opportunities, moods, and other unimagined commitments and actions follow.

An Honorable Tradition

You may think that surrender is the final act of defeat.

Perhaps you believe that surrender means you are somehow weak or powerless, ignorant or incapable of finding solutions to your problems.

It does not.

Surrender is the legitimate choice of warriors. Before going into battle with a noble adversary, samurai would surrender to the inevitability of their death. To resist or fear would distract them from the moment. And distraction assured defeat. Surrender as a "way of being" allowed these warriors to become masters of being present, living each moment with impeccability, and staying open to all possibilities. And surrender as a way of life enabled them to prevail more times than not.

In a real-time world, by the time we think about what's happening, what we are thinking about has already passed. Frustration, anxiety, resentment, resignation, denial: these moods show up when we cannot keep up with how fast the game is unfolding, when we encounter things and people we cannot control, or when we confront the limits of our current capabilities.

Think of surrender as an honest acknowledgment that we simply cannot control many, if not most, aspects of life. Think of surrender as the kind of profound acceptance that Eastern philosophies speak of as the key to serenity.

Say "Yes"

Surrender is an action. It is also how we relate to our circumstances.

The action of saying *yes* to life can be exercised at every moment of our lives. We can live in a state of surrender by being present and allowing of what is, by noticing circumstances and accepting them, by connecting with other people and accepting them too. We can declare that we trust life.

Surrender is a way of working *with* life.

Sometimes we find ourselves struggling indefinitely with a problem. By letting go of whatever we have been holding onto or resisting (including the "unsolvable" problem), we make space to think thoughts that were previously unthinkable. When we surrender to the fact that we've exhausted all possible solutions and that the problem may be unsolvable, we often see something we didn't see before—and that something allows us to create a totally unforeseen solution.

Surrender is at the heart of the human capacity to create. To create a new reality, we first surrender to the reality we have already created.

When we engage with reality *as it emerges* (rather than resist or resign ourselves to it), we realize that there are no "messes" to be cleaned up. Everything is as it is.

Everything is part of our game.

A Choice

Surrender is a choice that is always available to us, regardless of our circumstances.

Choosing is a creative act. In a real-time world, living in the future or the past is living disconnected from the present. Choosing only happens in the present.

Choosing is a commitment.

To choose is not the same as to make a decision. The process of deciding, which is usually based in reason, may or may not involve surrendering control or creating new possibilities. Choosing involves accepting reality as it is, intentionally creating a possible future, and committing to move into action to realize it.

When we reason, we typically are weighing alternatives or options and concluding that one is preferable to another. We might, for example, be in a dilemma, having to decide between going to the beach or doing some work. *Deciding* to go to the beach doesn't mean we do it. Deciding alone doesn't move us into action. Once we *commit* to what we have decided, we have made a choice. When we choose, we are already in action. The evidence of our choice is that we are driving to the beach.

We often confuse deciding (thinking) with choosing (being in action). This becomes apparent when we're dealing with addictions or unproductive habits like procrastination. The alcoholic or the procrastinator may "decide" to stop or modify their drinking or procrastinating. But the nature of their addiction or their habit overpowers their decisions: it controls them. When we think we control something which we don't, that "something" will control us. In Bill Wilson's "The Big Book" (*Alcoholics Anonymous: The Story of How Many Thousands of Men and Women Have Recovered from Alcoholism*), this condition is referred to as a disease of self-centeredness.[2] No matter what the alcoholic thinks, decides, or wishes, they will continue to drink until they hit bottom and confront the fact that they have no control. They must realize that they cannot "think" a commitment, that they have lost the ability to choose, and that they cannot recover by themselves.

Choice and control are not just subjects for alcoholics and procrastinators. We are all susceptible to believing that our perceptions and feelings about the world are true and accurate accounts of the way it really is. Gregory Bateson, Francisco Varela, and others have observed this phenomenon of thinking inside the context of our personal and cultural worldview and refer to it as the "self-referential" mind. Most of us can easily find instances in which we thought we were in control or "right" about our point of view, only to discover that we were blind to something—and as soon as we "saw" what we hadn't seen before, another viewpoint suddenly appeared to us and changed our life. We realized that "reality" isn't what we think it is and is always showing up in the context of our historical and cultural interpretation. This is why what is "real" for one person is not "real" for another.

In a real-time world, the idea of *choosing reality to be whatever it is* can help remind us to stop resisting and stop thinking that we know more than we do, to start accepting and committing to what is happening every moment and relating to our perceptions and experience with a sense of wonder and appreciation. To surrender is to choose life on life's terms, to go with the flow and be open to navigating the unpredictable.

When we surrender control of life, we frequently experience the emergence of a strong "faith" in something *outside ourselves* and also discover a new and powerful relationship *with ourselves*. Religious conversions and 12-Step Programs, for instance, often involve surrendering some element of our self to the promise and possibility of a "new way" or connection with a "higher power".

I've learned through my own experience that choosing is not an act of individual will. It's an act that becomes possible only in a relationship with something outside myself. This relationship allows me to suspend or give up control. This is because a relationship with something separate from myself—something that is not "me" (it could be Nature, the Universe, science, or an ideology, for example)—changes the perspective, and that change in perspective allows for the creation of something that was previously missing or unavailable. This is why I believe that acceptance or surrender is an essential first step towards being continuously present in a real-time world.

Serene Ambition

Surrender can become a way of being. And, like most aspects of living in a real-time world, it invites us to play with paradox and possibility.

Becoming comfortable with paradox is one of the most difficult aspects of mastering acceptance. Rather than relating to whatever we're thinking about in an "either/or" way, we include whatever we're resisting and formulate a "both/and" approach. Every action involves both short *and* long-term implications. Every commitment we make has an upside *and* a downside. People are both fine the way they are *and* they are always capable of more. We can be 100% committed at work *and* at home.

For instance, Mahatma Gandhi led India to independence through non-violent civil disobedience as a political strategy. He was surrendered to the fact that he could not win self-rule by arms or violence in the face of a much more powerful force, while at the same time he was committed to the possibility of civil rights and freedom.

We can learn to live in a state of permanent acceptance of ourselves, of other people, of what is occurring and the way things are. And, at the same time, we can generate possible futures and commit to our dreams of having satisfying, meaningful lives and achieving our ambitions for success.

Change is a constant. And in many areas of life it is accelerating in pace. Increasingly, we can no longer trust our predictions of what will happen based on our past knowledge and experience. Instead, we can develop an awareness of emerging possibilities, as well as the ability to make bold, risky commitments. We can learn to surf the waves of emerging reality and master the art of being in the moment. We can live as if everything is perfect the way it is—*and* as if there is always a larger possibility.

I call this paradoxical way of moving in the world, this surrender-commitment (simultaneously surrendering and committing), "Serene Ambition".

Serene Ambition offers us a basic orientation for relating to just about everything in a real-time world. If we are not clear about what's happening in the present or if we have no intention for the future, then we are basically lost and adrift. Four points summarize how we can cultivate surrender-commitment as a capability for navigating effectively in real time:

1. Don't react or resist what is.
2. Be clear about our commitments.

3. Observe what is missing.

4. Create what is possible.

Living in the apparent paradox between accepting what's going on in the present while still being responsible for whatever future we are committed to is essentially a matter of integrity, of experiencing one's self as whole and complete. Integrity in this sense is a kind of rigorous honesty, which has been captured in this popular version of the Serenity Prayer.

"God, grant me the serenity to accept the things I cannot change, courage to change the things I can, and wisdom to know the difference."[3]

No Nonsense

Serene Ambition is a rigorous, no nonsense way of being.

Living in a state of continual acceptance in each and every moment requires rigorous honesty. Some things fall away. Rationalizing and justifying whatever prior conversations we were holding onto to maintain the illusion that some desired outcome was possible when it is not becomes pointless.

Habits, such as procrastination or anxiety about the future, evaporate. Learning to live in the present takes away the power and, frequently, the domination of the narratives and stories that feed into these negative behaviors and recurring moods. When we are responsible for a future that we are creating, we are much more able to let go of their embodied nature. In most cases, when Serene Ambition becomes a way of life, many such habits and recurring moods simply disappear.

Other things take their place.

We develop the **capacity to be complete**—to be present—in every moment. Being complete is not the same as being finished. Finished is a function of the circumstances and the rules of whatever game we were playing. Completion is a state of being and the freedom to engage with many contingencies and move in almost any direction in any moment. As every professional coach knows, one of the primary functions in the role of a coach is to help the players on the team be complete (that is, let go of the past and their stories and be present and open in every moment of the game).

When accepting life the way it is, we don't need to traffic in the story about why. Causality is a child of the linear world—not the exponential. Acceptance implies just getting the way it is.

We often experience a **profound sense of humility, gratitude, and appreciation** for the mysterious vastness of the Universe that is always beyond the boundaries of human comprehension.

However, with surrender comes **vulnerability**.

Vulnerability

To be vulnerable is to authentically acknowledge our real lack of control over most things in our life, including other human beings. Being vulnerable does not mean we are powerless. On the contrary. Anyone who has ever been at a meeting when an infant is in the room will know that the baby has enormous power to get people's attention. Yet they are the most vulnerable person in the room.

Serene Ambition, this art of surrender, casts us as vulnerable adults committed to larger possibilities. Acknowledging our vulnerability, while being in a state of acceptance, can connect us with the experience of being sufficient to create and, ultimately, win new games. Rather than struggle with our circumstances, we can face the immediacy of life and embrace the fact that we are always in the moment and any action we take will also always be in the moment.

Serene Ambition allows us to surf the waves of emergent reality, not as hapless victims of disruption, but as fully empowered human beings using whatever is available in the present as raw material for creating our future. Serene Ambition embraces each moment with appreciation, a sense of wonder and, perhaps even, awe at the mysteries and unknowables of life.

"Vulnerability is not weakness,
and the uncertainty, risk, and emotional exposure
we face every day are not optional."
Brené Brown[4]

Chapter 3

BEING:
the art of context

We are used by context: the only question (and choice) is which context will use us.

Why Context?

Our way of being is the context within which we relate to the world. The question is what context—what way of being—will help us navigate.

In our quest for progress, everything today is being disrupted.

Disruption is, essentially, change that we didn't expect. Change for which we did not plan. It is large-scale, unprecedented, and permanent.

Disruptive change can give us many of the things we say we want, especially access to products and ways of doing things that are not only much better, faster, and cheaper than ever before, but also much more sustainable and environmentally and socially responsible. But there is always a cost for getting more of what we want. We're still discovering what many of these costs might be. At a minimum, they involve letting go of the known and familiar. Even more profound, they involve challenging and perhaps giving up our most cherished and taken-for-granted assumptions about ourselves, who we are as individuals, and what it means to be a human being.

The most challenging assumptions we have to deal with are those that objectify who we are and lock us into stories about why we are that way. If you and another person, using the same facts of your life, were to write two radically different stories, which would be true? Living in a real-time world involves acknowledging that our life stories are not true or false, but are interpretations which can either empower and inspire or limit and suppress possibility.

New fundamental principles of sharing, inter-dependency, and transparency are associated with many of the changes emerging in our society. Similarly, the fundamentals of our historical way of being are being driven towards innovation, evolution, and change. Disruption invites us to give up the certainty and predictability of the status quo, the comfort and naïveté of old habits, and the constancy and control of outdated common sense. It urges us to embrace the competency of accepting. And disruption specifically calls us to question our way of being—our persona—to consider that the way we are is a choice.

This is not easy. We live in a condition of cognitive blindness. Just as water is transparent to a fish, our way of being is normally self-referential and transparent to us. This is often obvious to people who have been transported from one culture to another: they realize how their way of observing, their basic assumptions, and their reactions are radically different when put into a different context. It's in these situations, when we move from a familiar to an unfamiliar environment, that we can become conscious and aware that the "way we are" is *not* a given. It is a dynamic function of our interdependence with everyone and everything around us.

We learn or develop through trial and practice a basic "presentation" as young adults and then spend our lives living out this "story" and the way we are and why we got this way. This *self* that we show the world, although it might *seem* authentic, actually objectifies who we are and often leaves us feeling slightly disconnected from ourselves and others as we begin to move into "life disrupted". If we look back at a photo of ourselves from ten years ago and reflect on our experience then and how we understand our world now, there is often a radical difference. What happened? Did the world change—or do we now have a deeper understanding of who we are and what our values are today as opposed to yesterday?

As the rate and scope of change speeds up, our historical stories and ways of being may no longer work and may even be counter-productive. For example, if we see ourselves as a hard worker and believe the secret to success lies in lots of preparation, we will probably work harder and do even more of whatever we can to prepare ourselves *even when we notice that what we are doing is not producing the results we desire.*

We learned to construct a story about the "way we are" in our youth. We can also learn to construct a story about who we are now and about who we intend to be in the future. In a real-time world, we need to cultivate this capability of continuously reinventing ourselves and our story in ways that are both effective and authentic.

Most of us will acknowledge that we are not the same person we were a decade or two ago. Constructing new stories about who we are being is a matter of observing, re-interpreting what we observe, and then taking action. The self-reinvention process—the journey of self-mastery— starts with cultivating new practices so we can simply observe and not react. These new practices, outlined throughout the chapters in this book, are about cultivating capabilities we already have—not about learning new concepts and trying to apply them.

As seen in the previous chapter, we all have the ability to accept or resist. We also have the capability to distinguish between context and content, having a lifetime of experience at grasping context before language (and thereby giving specific words specific meanings). In situations where we are dealing with an immediate and urgent crisis, we are able to learn in the moment whatever we need to learn to prevail. We each have had the experience of being able to observe and report on our moods and then act and perform independent of them so that they do not negatively impact the quality of our work or our performance. And anyone who has been part of a powerful partnership or team is able to see how inseparable communication and relationship actually are.

One interpretation of who we are being that could be useful is that we are our relationships with: 1) our "ego" (internal self-talk), 2) others, 3) our circumstances, 4) time, and 5) a higher power (or whatever is beyond our comprehension). Generating a relationship with something outside or beyond our understanding (what I call "otherness") is important: it is what allows us to transcend our point of view so that we don't have to remain trapped in a self-referential relationship with our point of view.

We are a product of whatever context we choose to relate to each of these relationships in. For instance, if we relate to time as a finite resource, we may become time managers, watching over and carefully controlling our use of "it". If we relate to time as a variable that is dependent upon on our commitments, we can become focused prioritizers, dancing with the ebb and flow of life as it arises. Similarly, if we look at our circumstances from a context of them being fixed, objective things, we will naturally react or attempt to control. If we look at our circumstances from the context of responsibility for how we perceive, we will naturally work *with* circumstances to accomplish our objectives.

Using the framework of these five relationships makes it possible to be more dynamic, flexible, and authentic in how we relate and respond to life as it unfolds. In a real-time world, being authentic can be understood as owning our historical way of being, as well as having our inner experience and commitments aligned and consistent. It involves learning to break free of our habitual patterns and beginning to distinguish and generate the contexts within which we live and observe the world. That is, the process of self-reinvention starts with not only not reacting, but also with learning to observe ourselves and consciously accept and choose however we are being and whatever we are experiencing in the moment (including our moods as expressions of our way of being) while, at the same time, becoming sufficiently aware that our historical way of being may no longer be serving our commitments.

We are always expressing who we are in the world. We do so with every word we speak and every item we choose to wear, with the approach we take to each set of circumstances and with the ways we choose to relate to the people we meet. **We all have the capacity to choose to *be* any way we want to be in every moment.** Navigating real time successfully is a matter of exercising our innate capability to continuously transform our relationships with ourselves and others, with our circumstances and time, with everything in our reality and with that which is beyond our comprehension.

I Think, Therefore I Am

This notion has shaped our ideas about what it means to be human. I am a thinking thing or a thing that thinks.

First articulated by René Descartes, the father of modern Western philosophy, in 1637, this declaration ushered in an entirely new worldview.[1] This groundbreaking concept of the self has given us the field of psychology and the science of how these things called human beings work. It has given us the field of management and the study of how to control and motivate these human resources. It has given us beliefs about what it means to be a man or a woman, what it means to be a good or bad person, and what it means to be any of a hundred other attributes or distinctions that have come down to us through our culture.

Over the next 350 years or so, this concept of the self as an object has evolved to become a central part of our history and our culture. As a practical matter, we now view who we are as a more or less fixed psychological entity consisting of a personality and an "ego", as well as personal beliefs, traits, and strengths. We think of ourselves in terms of human "resources". We do tests to define and label our leadership style or personality type.

We use these assessments and other objective criteria to guide how we go about building our relationships. And most of us, unconsciously and consciously, develop and live out various patterns for either projecting or protecting the self that we consider ourselves to be.

Yet are we, essentially, just things that think?

Constant & Unchangeable

This interpretation of the self as object has us believe
that who we are is more or less constant and unchangeable,
that we have a predetermined personality that defines us
and makes us unique. Living in this worldview of the self
as object traps us in fixed interpretations of our moods and
our attitudes, actions, and behaviors.

After all, if we are objects, then we need to look good
and have a lot of good things going for us. We have to prove
our worth and defend what we think. We cover up any
flaws we think we have or compensate for them to compete
or, in some cases, to survive. We search inside ourselves,
gain some insights and more self-awareness. And if we
don't like what we find, then it is time to "work on
ourselves". The practices of self-awareness tend to focus
on a deeper appreciation of the "way we are" as a fixed
psychological entity.

We invest a good portion of our lives chasing the myth
that there is an objective "me" that can be explored and
developed. I prefer to think that whoever we are or
consider ourselves to be only lives in our conversations.
And the loudest, most prominent conversation is the one
we have with ourselves. That internal conversation is

actually a historical story made up of assessments and gives us the illusion of constancy. Assessments, however, are neither true nor false: they are our conclusions and interpretations, not the facts. Most of us forget the difference. We hold our assessments to be true and so we believe our story about who we are.

Do we want our life story to have us—or do we want to have a life story?

The answer depends on how we understand causality. If we believe our story is an accurate account of **how** and **why** things are the way they are, then we become trapped in that historical interpretation. If we believe that commitments and actions cause our situation and our world to be the way they are, then we can have many stories based in the same facts (the "**what**").

Control

This historical notion of self as object comes with a parallel idea: if we view ourselves as constant, then we tend to view life and our circumstances as variable. In order to prevail and get what we want, we typically assume we must have control over our lives and our circumstances.

We make most of our choices and measure most of our decisions inside this thinking. We lean towards predictability in the hope it will help us minimize risk, maintain stability, manage growth. We try to predict outcomes based on what we do or do not control and on what we *think* we can or cannot control. We try to manage change and circumstances just as vigorously as we try to manage people and processes.

We turn "what works" in terms of controlling ourselves and others into recipes and formulas and silver bullets. And yet humans are not *things*. Humans are *beings*. We cannot know with much degree of certainty what human beings, individually or collectively, will choose next. Therefore, we cannot trust our predictions or our formulas when it comes to human activities—and that covers everything from elections and terrorist threats to stock markets and national economies.

Control—whether it is of human behaviors, mechanical processes, or unforeseen circumstances—always
involves resistance. Without resistance, there is nothing to
control. When we resist something, we become a party to
its persistence. When we believe we need to have control
to get what we want, we become the source of what it is we
say we don't want.

One of the distinguishing features of our real-time
world is its very unpredictability. We can no longer rely on
the past when approaching the future. Instead we need to
accept and embrace unpredictability as a fact of life and
shift the question from "What will happen?" to "What are
we committed to make happen?" Further, how do we
relate to the future when we can't control it? How do we
relate to ourselves and each other when we cannot control
or predict what will happen?

Yesterday's pace of slow change meant we had time to
adapt to our place in our environment. But in a real-time
world, change is happening faster and faster: adaptation is
a process that often happens too slowly to keep up. Today's
much faster pace of change often has us experiencing
anxiety, a sense of being out of touch, an impression that
we are losing control. Whenever our environment and our
place in it changes faster than the pace we have become

used to, we are at risk of becoming, or at least feeling, obsolete.

Fast change means we need to cultivate the ability to alter our relationship with our environment. With this competency, we can change who we are *and* our environment. Without it, we can end up trapped in a habitual way of being that no longer works and in a relationship with a reality that no longer exists.

Since we can no longer fall back on predictability and control, we can surrender and go with the flow *and* also create a new reality. If we choose to create a new reality, we have to learn new skills such as "how fast can you reinvent who you are" as a continuous process of relating to what is happening. Developing this particular skill will help us create a new relationship to whatever is emerging *as it emerges* in real time.

We essentially need to cultivate our ability to create new ways of being and contexts which distinguish our relationships with everything in our world. Being aware that we have a choice in how we relate to what is happening invites the possibility of being serene and centered and focused, regardless of what's occurring. When we forget that we have this choice, the barriers to cultivating new ways of being bring us back to our addiction to, beliefs about, and history of being controllers.

Creating does not come from the mechanical and the repetitive, the reactive or the resistant. Creating does not come from control. (The notion that we control creativity is a non sequitur at best, nonsensical at worst.)

Life in a real-time world is essentially a continuous, never-ending creative process of relating to life as possibility.

This can be a difficult idea to get our heads around. Every moment is a new creation that is informed by history and tradition. We can "be here now", living in the immediacy of the present moment, a moment informed by and connected to our past but not limited or determined by it. We can respect and be responsible for our history while we, in the same instant, explore new possible futures and head in new directions.

We can simply keep reinventing ourselves.

The Individual & The Collective

Our commonsense idea of "self" is essentially a combination of two historical stories. One, the story or belief we as an individual hold about ourselves. And two, the collective story we hold about what it is to be a human being.

We are our shared collective story and our individual stories. And yet we are not necessarily either. We did not choose these stories. They are a product of our culture, traditions, and historical practices. Once we understand they are *interpretations* and realize we do not have to take them for granted as truths, we then have a choice in how we relate to ourselves and the world. The fact that our reality is always occurring in the context of our historical narrative doesn't mean that the narrative is trivial or not central to our existence. We are always living within some interpretation or another. The question is are we aware that none of these narratives is true—or false—and that we have a choice with respect to what story or narrative we choose for our lives.

We have been and still are simultaneously evolving, creating, and living our interpretations of what it is to be a human being.

Some collective narratives that originated in the Middle Ages and the Renaissance about who we are (e.g., the distinction between body and soul) and what we see as being humanly possible (e.g., individuation and perspective) are still taken-for-granted aspects of how we see the world today. Other narratives have disappeared, only to be replaced by some of the modern and new ideas that are constantly emerging. For instance, a social media app changed the meaning of "friend". We question where the boundaries of "being human" lie as the distinction between biology and technology blurs with reproductive cloning and neural lace networks. Are we animals? Are we some symbiosis of biology and machine? Small wonder we are having to create new ethics to deal with what is getting stirred up in our real-time existence.

We create and evolve our individual interpretations of who we are by declaration. A declaration is a commitment that something is the way it is because we say so. As individuals, we can declare ourselves "**to be**..." and finish the sentence with just about anything we are fully committed to being. With this declaration, we make a choice and a commitment to being the way we say we are.

But that declaration alone doesn't change who we are or our circumstances. It can change the *relationship* between who we say we are and our circumstances. It can change how we *listen*. It can change how we *observe* our world. And *that* can change what is possible for us. For example, it can open the possibility for learning or inventing new practices, new tools, new conversations and, in the final analysis, new realities.

Consider that, when we relate to what is happening within the context of our commitment "to be _____", we can observe anything that is inconsistent with who we say we are as an opportunity for learning and for change. That inconsistency shows up as an opening for reflection and new commitment, rather than as a fault or weakness. This can allow us to inquire into the question of "What's missing?" for us to change, rather than "What's wrong with me?" or "What's wrong with whatever I believe is limiting me?". In turn, this opens up possibilities and choices previously not available to us.

Reinvention

As George Bernard Shaw so aptly put it, "Life isn't about *finding* yourself. Life is about *creating* yourself...."[2]

Language and committed action are the keys to reinventing who we are.

We invent ourselves by declaring who we are. We become ourselves by following up those declarations with committed actions.

We are who we say we are if and only if:

1. We are committed to what we say, and
2. We walk the talk (in other words, our actions express our commitments).

Life in a real-time world calls us to be present, to be authentic, and to make conscious choices about how we will respond in a given moment. Whether we are playing a game, performing a song, painting a masterpiece, or doing our job, being present in this way is preferable to being on auto pilot, moving through life either stuck in a reactive mode or simply unconscious of our choices.

Reinvention, then, is the competency to repeatedly recreate who we are *while staying present and relevant and in action in the moment.*

Creating New Ways of Being

Creating new ways of being involves changing how we observe and relate to the world.

Life in a real-time world calls us to respond, not react. Yet most people most of the time are reacting to life—not responding—based on their story about themselves and their beliefs about how they *and* life "should be".

This thinking brings us back, once again, to the interpretation that we are objects or things. If we believe life happens *to* us, we, therefore, do everything we can to learn how to control what happens in order to succeed or we at least learn how to react skillfully. We can win if "who we are" has all the right stuff (looks, pedigree, power, resources, intelligence, and so on). If not, we probably succumb to our inner critic, that little voice in our heads that is always prompting us to strive for "more, better, and different" variations of what we have or who we think we are or should be. Of course, if we're not into striving, then we end up settling for whatever life gives us.

If we believe we are things, then changing ourselves becomes very difficult. Change usually gets associated with some major event—a crisis or a revelation or "hitting bottom".

While it is true we have bodies and our brains and nervous systems are remarkable in terms of managing our behavior, we are not just a physical thing. We are also creative beings capable of both making original choices and taking actions that seem counter-intuitive to us, like ignoring consensus, loving our enemies, and seeking out what we fear most. Our choices, however, are always limited to what is available in whatever interpretation we have of who we are.

Is there an interpretation of who we are that could remove these limits?

I Am My Relationships

I answer the "Who am I?" question with a declaration: "I am my relationships." This offers me enormous freedom and power in how I experience life and the choices I make.

By relationships, I mean much more than just my relationships with other people. Five relationships constitute "who I am". Specifically, my relationships with:

- My ego (self-talk)
- Others
- Circumstances
- Time
- Otherness (or God, the Universe, Nature, Spirit— essentially, what is beyond the limits of my comprehension and understanding).

For me, self-mastery is choosing to *be* present and responsive in all of these fundamental domains of relationship. I believe that I would cease to exist if any of them were missing. Just as Descartes could not imagine existing independent of his thinking, I cannot imagine existing in the absence of these five constitutive relationships.

These five relationships form the context of my life: they constitute the space in which the world occurs for me. They are like the facets of who I am—a beautiful prism through which I can observe, organize, and respond (rather than react) to my reality.

Response-ability

I don't have control over most of the circumstances of my life or what happens. I do, however, always have a choice about how I **relate** to those circumstances and events.

No matter what the situation, when I change how I relate to myself, others, my circumstances, time, or otherness, I perceive everything differently. Therefore, I am *being* a different person in that situation.

All of us have experienced being one way with our family or friends and being another way with our employer or colleagues at work. We normally don't question these differences in our way of being. We don't examine our assumptions. We play our roles out of habit and justify them as more or less culturally defined norms.

But in a real-time world, we are living in the moment, surfing the emerging waves of life. We need to be **responsive** to *whatever* is happening. To be responsive, we need to be able to consciously choose how to relate to what is happening in the moment. To be responsive, we have to be responsible (that is, response-able). This applies in all of the five relationships: with ego, with others, with circumstances, with time, and with otherness.

Our choice is always to *accept* or *resist*, to surrender or not. For instance, if my computer breaks down the day before I leave for a business trip and I resist what's happening, I get overwhelmed and stressed about not having enough time to complete all my work. If instead I can accept the fact of the breakdown, I can focus on what my priorities are and respond by being in action.

When we resist, we are reacting.

When we accept, we are able to be present. When we are present, we are able to consciously choose how we listen and how we respond.

We are able to choose who we are.

Being Your Word

"I am my word."

It took me many years of living to come to this conclusion. After all, I experience my life in and through language. I don't merely describe an objective world with my words. Over time, I also create the world I'm describing through speaking—and listening to—conscious and unconscious commitments uttered every day.[3] In addition, I use language to shape and reinforce my worldview. And my worldview shapes how I perceive reality.

What I say, therefore, makes a difference.

What happens, for instance, when I say, "I love you"? Or when I ask for your help? Or when I pass judgment on your work and promise to meet you to discuss it tomorrow? In all these cases, I am using speaking and listening to create our future.

When we can see that our life occurs in conversations and language, we can appreciate the importance of being rigorous and authentic about how we listen and what we say. The difference between the endless spewing of opinions and a powerful and effective conversation is commitment. Are we clear what other people mean when they speak? Do *we* mean what we say and say what we mean? We call this skill set committed speaking and committed listening.

Throughout most of human history, a person's word was their bond. Honor came before glory. Promises and declarations were commitments that were taken very seriously: we knew there would be serious consequences if we didn't do what we said we would. In some cases, we lived and died by our word. In a real-time world, we have less and less room for misunderstandings. In a real-time world, the consequences of living with unexamined assumptions or being unconscious about our worldview can be severe.

Committed speaking and listening are crucial for a real-time navigator.

Existential Confidence

Because we can't predict the future or trust our past to guide us, it's important that we have confidence in ourselves to believe that we are equal and sufficient to whatever is emerging. We call this "existential confidence", or self-trust in our way of being. Confidence in who we are.

This is about having enough confidence in myself and my way of being in the world that I can make unpredictable and unreasonable promises and trust I will be able to deliver—even if I don't know how and have never made or kept such a promise before. This existential confidence shows up as an authentic belief that I am sufficient to create whatever is necessary to deliver promises that are outside of what I have delivered in the past.

Confidence is an expression of my relationship with myself. Confidence in my way of being is distinct from other confidences I may have about myself. I may, for example, be confident in my skills—everything from golfing and driving to solving problems and speaking in public. I may be confident in my ability to earn and manage money. Or confident in the efficacy of my work relationships. But confidence in my way of being is neither a skill nor an ability I can "acquire".

Being existentially confident is about moving in the world with intentionality and a sense of personal agency. It shows up in how I comport myself when I enter a conversation, how I stay centered in chaos, how I meet uncertainty with calm. It is reflected in my capacity to commit to a possibility before there is any evidence that it is possible and in my willingness to be open and vulnerable while I courageously put myself and my identity on the line as I make big promises and take big risks.

This way of being in relationship—confident, calm, open, centered, courageous—works for pioneers and innovators, engineers and artists, leaders and followers. Existential confidence, combined with committed action, makes the difference between just having a good idea and succeeding in the face of extraordinary challenges. It is, therefore, important in any field of human endeavor in our real-time world.

The Entrepreneurial Self

Reinventing our way of being in relationship to our real-time world is closely connected with entrepreneurship.

One of the most universal and challenging issues we face today is the "future of work". Most serious thinking on the subject suggests that as much as 50% of the population may be unemployed by 2050. Regardless of what predictions say, a lot of people around the world are already either unemployed or underemployed. And of those who *are* employed, a mere 15% are actively engaged with what they are doing.[4]

When it comes to figuring out how to make a living, most people have tended to concentrate on two things: what they can do and what they like. They then package whatever they think has value from this combination and try to sell it. As technology advances at an accelerating rate, however, work itself is changing. Jobs go obsolete almost overnight. Required skills and knowledge keep shifting, almost faster than our education systems can adjust. The gig economy is growing. At the same time, more and more individuals want to make a commitment to do work that has meaning for them, work that is interesting and that, in some way, takes care of something that concerns them or that concerns someone they care about.

We are always creating our reality, just as we are always co-creating our shared future. We take care of others by taking care of ourselves. And we help ourselves by helping others. We are both autonomous human beings and inseparably and indivisibly part of humanity: we are always both a part *and* the whole. We have lived with this paradox between the individual and the collective since we began forming communities.

One way I frequently express this paradox is with the idea that only an individual can commit, but no individual can fulfill a commitment of any consequence by themselves.

This is essentially what entrepreneurs do, whether they work on freelance projects as solopreneurs or hire others to do the work that needs to be done in their private enterprise. They commit to taking care of concerns. From this perspective, everyone has the capability to be entrepreneurial. Entrepreneurs are ordinary people who look around for what is needed and wanted in the world and then go about figuring how to provide it. They listen to what people's concerns are, anticipate what they will be in the future, and then make offers to take care of those concerns. They are often at the bleeding edge of emerging trends. They choose to bring a new enterprise into existence in the face of established markets, fierce competition, and historical expectations and patterns of consumption—often with insufficient resources and at the expense of friends and family. Success depends on the entrepreneur's ability to take care of the needs of all who have a stake in the enterprise's sustainability—from clients, customers, and employees to suppliers, board members, and investors.

One of the first people I listened to as a mentor said something I've never forgotten. "Entrepreneurs have only one measure for success: their results. Being an entrepreneur isn't something you do. It's just a label, a label you can call yourself *after* you've been successful in bringing a new enterprise into existence."

I think of entrepreneurs as existential warriors.

Entrepreneurs stand apart in the face of adversity, resistance and, sometimes, almost super-human challenges. They are willing to dance on the razor's edge between passion and fear, always pushing forward, often unreasonably, in the face of a common sense that says, "This will *never* work...". They do not go into the game to see who will win. Instead, they bring their vision of victory and success with them into every encounter. They have the courage to stay the course when more reasonable people would choose a safer and more comfortable path.

Being a successful entrepreneur has as much to do with who you are as it does with what you know or what you are offering. Besides being passionate and fearless, these existential warriors demonstrate a bedrock of commitment that makes them easy to trust. This 1980s Shearson/American Express advertisement expresses this character well:

"Commitment is what transforms a promise into reality. It is the words that speak boldly of your intentions. And the actions that speak louder than the words.

It is making the time when there is none. Coming through time after time after time, year after year after year.

Commitment is the stuff character is made of; the power to change the face of things.

It is the daily triumph of integrity over skepticism."

Chapter 4

LISTENING:
the art of mastering moods

Before we meet, before anyone speaks, even before we think, we are already listening—and we are always navigating in the context our listening provides.

Why Mastering Moods?

Before we could speak, we listened.

Before words and language even had meaning for us, we listened.

We listened to relate to and make sense of whatever was happening in our world. This was not simply a matter of hearing sounds, although we did do that. And it was not just a matter of decoding words or processing information.

I think of listening as conscious awareness. We listen with all of our senses and cognitive capacity. Listening is an all-encompassing, universal phenomenon. Listening is what organizes and correlates our relationships with our selves, others, circumstances, time, and whatever is beyond our comprehension.

In a relatively stable world, our listening tends to be generally structured by our past experiences, expectations, beliefs, and prejudices. We come into almost every situation listening through this set of filters. These filters color our interpretations of whatever is said—or not said— and inform the meanings we give to certain circumstances and behaviors. In other words, we are always already listening. This structure of interpretation, sometimes called our "already listening", shows up in our stories and our automatic reactions, our patterns of thinking and our moods.

Listening is not the same as hearing. Hearing is perceiving sound; listening is interpreting the meaning of those sounds. We may, therefore, hear the same words without necessarily listening the same meaning.

We are not limited to passive, automatic listening. We can alter how we listen—and, therefore, how we relate—by committing to listen in particular ways. Instead of listening to someone and then reacting to whatever we are hearing, we can listen **for** something. "Listening for" is a way to focus and pay attention to what others are saying as a function of our concerns or the purpose or context of a particular conversation.

When I was newly married, my wife would constantly criticize my driving. I heard it as nagging and would get defensive. Whenever we were going someplace in the car, the mood would be tense and heavy. One day, when we were enduring a ride together, I decided to shift how I was relating to what was happening. So I asked myself, "Where is the nagging?" I realized that the nagging was happening not in her words, but in my listening. I had been "already listening" through a filter, a set of egocentric assessments of myself as a good driver combined with the belief that anyone who is critical of me and how I drive is clearly attacking me and, therefore, creating a problem for me.

I made a commitment to change how I listened. I chose to interpret every criticism she had of my driving as her way of saying, "I love you." (This private conversation with myself was something I never shared with her.) When she would criticize me, I would acknowledge her assessments by saying, "Thank you" or "I understand." I didn't react or resist her view. I would just keep listening for her love. Within a few days of this new listening on my part, she stopped criticizing my driving entirely. The mood in the car shifted almost as if by magic and, as far as I can recall, I didn't change how I was driving.

Changing how we listen not only can impact the experience and behaviors of others. It can also intervene in our moods and how we observe and experience life.

Moods may be the most ubiquitous and constitutive aspect of being human. Our moods give meaning to our experience and behaviors in much the same way the soundtrack of a movie brings a story to life. They are a principal factor in how we listen and how our world occurs for us on a moment-to-moment basis. And moods connect us in time and space with our past, present, and future.

Our listening always correlates with our moods.

Most of us normally associate our moods with our feelings. We tend to think of them psychologically and habitually try to explain why we are feeling a particular way or why we are in a particular mood, as if that is the pathway to resolving the negative ones and maintaining the positives. This focuses our attention and thinking on causality, which rarely makes any difference in terms of how we are experiencing the moods, our behaviors, or how others are relating to us. Searching for causes, we become prisoners, simply waiting for our moods to pass if they are negative or trying to hold onto them if they are positive.

Viewing our moods as manifestations of our listening (which is, itself, a function of our biology, our history, and our relationships) gives us a way to change how we observe and relate to our world. Our moods become a reflection of the landscape we are navigating in life. We can learn to recognize and relate to them as a kind of mirror of "where we're coming from" and our way of being in the present. By becoming more aware of our already listening and developing our innate capability to generate listening that is appropriate to our commitments and what is occurring around us, we can learn how to sustain mostly positive moods, such as serenity, regardless of what is happening in the world.

In our real-time world, we are navigating a continuously emerging reality while being engaged in an ocean of our own and other people's listening, moods, and commitments. We can cultivate our capacity to listen to a broad spectrum of phenomenon, including what is being said and what is not being said, our body's responses and other people's responses, our moods and others' moods. We can literally become different observers. This more holistic way of observing can give us direct access to the context or "frame" within which we and others are moving through life. Having access to context opens up possibilities for action and unprecedented results. With access to the background or context of a situation, we can begin to shape how our worlds occur for us and engage and collaborate in more powerful conversations to create a common future.

Fully Present

What does it mean to be "fully present"?

Some of us experience being fully present when we are "in the zone", either playing sports, making music, or performing a task that calls for our undivided attention and focus. Many of us experience being fully present when we are in the midst of a crisis, in those moments or days when everything non-essential drops out of our awareness and our focus rests entirely on completing the task in front of us.

In this state of "being present", we think quickly and act decisively. The oncoming car is bearing down on us and our body responds instantaneously to swerve and avoid a head-on collision. The father finds out his wife and child are on the second floor of a burning building: he grabs a wet rag to cover his mouth and dashes into the smoke and flames. The lag time between something happening and our thinking and responding to it is minimal.

To navigate in real time means we are consistently— mind and body—*in* the present.

When we are fully in the present moment, we can use everything that is available to us through our conscious awareness and through our unconscious awareness to move appropriately within any situation. This way of navigating has us being responsible for the past, future, and present simultaneously. That is, we are being responsible for our interpretations of the past; responsible for our ambitions, expectations, and concerns for the future; responsible for what is needed and wanted, what is missing, and for what our relationships and moods, possibilities, and commitments are right now.

Today's dynamic reality requires that we stay fully present to what is happening—all the time—and that we remain simultaneously responsive and confident about our in-the-moment choices. When we become attached to our assumptions and our predictions or blinded by our prejudices and our already listening, we miss seeing emerging threats and opportunities. The consequences of such blindness in our real-time world can be severe and immediate.

> *"Realize deeply that the present moment is all you ever have. Make the NOW the primary focus of your life."*
> Eckhart Tolle[1]

Not Naïve

Not being fully present gives us, by default, our automatic already listening. Being fully present is the key to listening generatively.

Being fully present as we listen doesn't assume we ignore the past. Nor does it give us permission to be naïve about limitations we could face in the future. If anything, being present as part of the art of navigation requires that we learn to:

- Be responsible for the past and the future as contexts for our day-to-day choices
- Focus on and be prepared to challenge assumptions and beliefs that we have previously taken for granted.

Our assumptions and beliefs are usually transparent (that is, they can become blind spots). For the most part, we continue to take them for granted until they are revealed in the moments when we have a breakdown and get stopped as we try to fulfill our commitments. A breakdown is anything that thwarts or appears to thwart the realization of our intention. This connection between blind spots and breakdowns became particularly clear to me early in my career when I was thinking and writing about coaching as an alternative paradigm to traditional management. Coaching, which is always focused on action and possibility, happens through committed listening and speaking. One of the primary roles of the coach is to help people become aware of their blind spots in a way that can free them up to take new and, for them, unprecedented actions.

Coaching, like navigation, occurs in real time. Coaches don't go into a game with their team to see who wins. They enter into today's game coming from a committed interpretation of having already won. This allows them to be a different observer, to see what is missing to win in a particular moment of the game. What is missing can be almost anything: a perspective, a skill, a relationship, a commitment, a possibility, an action. During the game, the coach's role is not to criticize what a player has already done, but to communicate in a way that enables the player to take action to correct or provide something that is missing. In situations where action is the objective, there are no "right" or "wrong" circumstances, just what is actually happening in the moment and what is missing to achieve an objective.

Similarly, we can learn to navigate every aspect of life "as if" the future we've committed to has already been realized. Then we can observe what is missing in each moment and respond accordingly, rather than react to what is happening or paralyze ourselves in analysis about what happened in the past or what we think will or should happen in the future.

The Somatic Compass

Our body, or "the soma", acts as a compass in the present.

The fact is our physical body is always present in time and space. Arguably, it is the *only* aspect of ourselves that is fully present at every moment of our lives. Therefore, how we listen and relate to our body is a capability we can develop.

We so identify with our body—or not—that this relationship is often difficult to distinguish as a relationship. When we are healthy and happy, we might not even be aware of our soma. When we are "in our heads" being preoccupied with our own thinking, we are never quite 100% "in our body", aware of and present to our experience. Yet, when we break a limb or have a serious injury, it may seem as if our body is all there is.

In a real-time world, having a deep somatic awareness of where we are physically in time and space is more than simply good for us. The relationship we have with our body is a key to moving with confidence and clarity when we can't rely on the past or on thinking alone to inform our decisions. As navigators, we can begin to tune into this somatic compass by learning to listen to our physical sensations. Fortunately, there are entire fields of study and practice connected with expanding "body consciousness", "embodied wisdom", or "somatic awareness" to aid us in learning to how to listen and respond to what our body is telling us.

Mastering how to use our relationship with our bodies as a navigational tool, however, is about more than just listening to our gut and sensitizing ourselves to physical sensations. It is about becoming aware of the stories we have about what's happening in our bodies and in the environments through which our bodies move. It is about us remembering that, in a real-time world, there is very little time for us to "process" and analyze our stories.

For example, as an individual, I may have made up a story about the sharp, persistent pain I feel in my shoulder being associated with a trauma from my past. Trying to process my way out of that story and the mood of resignation that came with it can take weeks or months. Simply acknowledging that I have created a story that connects the physical pain I'm experiencing now with an unresolved emotional trauma from years ago can free me to choose alternative ways to relate to the pain. The story itself is neither true nor false. It is simply one possible interpretation.

I can choose that interpretation and the courses of action it opens to me. In some cases, just the awareness of having a choice can allow the body sensations to either change or disappear. In other cases, it can call for new choices. If the pain persists, I can engage someone to help me process the unexpressed feelings that appear to be contributing to my physical pain. Or I can accept the fact of my chronic pain and generate different possibilities in response to it. I can do my physiotherapy exercises, soak in the jacuzzi, meditate, book an acupuncture treatment or a massage. I can explore a combination of actions to address the problem in the moment—every time it occurs.

Tuning In

Listening is not a process. It is the context for what we normally mean by "awareness". It is a total sensory relationship with our external environment that has us not only aware of what is going on around us, but also aware of what is going on internally with us. This total sensory relationship—this "tuning in"—can allow us to become aware of our awareness.

The body is central to our existence. It is also central to our ability to navigate as a group in a rapidly changing world when we don't have the time to reflect, to analyze our best options, or to wait until someone else has an answer. When we are present in the moment, the body can be our most immediate and proximate source of information for navigating in real time. Listening to and trusting the body is what we're often referring to when we talk about trusting our gut or relying on our instincts, intuition, or feelings.

The emergence of a real-time world reveals what has always been, but which we have been cognitively blind to: namely, the paradox of the individual and the collective. We are now coming to grips with the idea that we are emerging as empowered, autonomous human individuals.

And, at the same time, we're also awakening to the permanent interconnectivity of all of us. The individual and the collective is no longer an either/or construct. Like the front and back of our hand, we can't have "individual" without the "collective" and we can't have the collective without individuals. Individual/collective is a whole context.

Traditionally, we've tended to objectify ourselves as individuals and, separately, objectify ourselves as individual members of collective structures (groups, organizations, communities, nations). Yet we are witnessing a dawning awareness of ourselves as the collective. As author Charles Eisenstein said, "We are not just a skin-encapsulated ego, a soul encased in flesh. We are each other and we are the world."[2]

Throughout history, leaders and sages have declared themselves to be more than merely individuals, just as philosophers have engaged with the question of what is a "self". As pointed out earlier, the idea that the self, who I am, is a fixed or objective thing no longer serves us well. The idea of the self as a *construct* which can become part of our shared understanding and practices, on the other hand, does. For example, the phrase "I am the nation" from Otto Whittaker Jr.'s poem by the same name has become a recognizable expression of American culture.[3]

In the 2017 film *Qaida Band*, seven prisoners sing, "I am, I am, I am, I am, I am India."[4] We can speak these phrases ("I am the nation", "I am India") as poetic or literal truths for ourselves. And, with our new awareness of the interbeing of all things, as Thich Nat Hanh has aptly called our interdependent co-existing, we can say them and *experience ourselves as the nation* or community.[5]

We human beings can and do experience the "collective body" in a myriad of different situations. For example, in the flow of traffic on our daily commute in Los Angeles and the flow of consumers through a shopping mall in Abu Dhabi. In the Asian team training for the next dragon boat festival and a challenger team playing in a virtual reality eSports competition. In the rapid mobilization of Canada's federal government during the Great Ice Storm of 1998, air traffic controllers around the world immediately after 9/11, and village communities impacted by the flooding in Fiji in 2012. Even mob behaviors, which can often be destructive, exemplify our ability to tune into a kind of collective consciousness and adjust our actions to move "as one".

Collective movements in both expected and unexpected situations do not necessarily require central coordination: they often emerge from some basic biological connection and learned behavioral rules that people and animals (such as insects, birds, fish, dogs, and horses) follow when they are in a group. That is, each individual:

- **Separates** themselves by keeping a certain distance away from their neighbors to avoid crowding
- **Aligns** with the general direction of their neighbors, and
- **Synchronizes** with their neighbors to achieve or maintain a desired future and protect the cohesiveness of the group.

These behaviors depend on individuals in the group unconsciously sensing what's going on with their own body (be it physical or virtual), the position and state of other nearby bodies, as well as what's in the space between bodies. People literally tune in to each other and to their environment, listening for dangers. They simultaneously maintain their individual autonomy and their connection to the group: another real-time paradox. This dynamic "attunement"—a combination of short-range repulsion, alignment, and long-range attraction—keeps everyone moving together as a group while minimizing risk and maximizing safety, avoiding threats and seizing opportunities.

This paradoxical relationship between the individual and the community demonstrates the fact that, while individuals make commitments, we can only fulfill our commitments by coordinating with others.

In a typical Alcoholics Anonymous® business meeting, for example, no one is in charge. No one individual exercises authority over what happens. Everyone attending goes with the "consciousness of the group" present at that specific meeting and moves together to take care of who and what needs to be taken care of. The welfare of the group comes first. Each individual commits to sobriety and accepts that they can't keep that commitment without the support of others. However, they are no longer merely individuals collaborating at the level of the individual to carry out their shared purpose: they are individually collaborating, coordinating, and cooperating *"in a fellowship"* to bring the A.A. message to the individual alcoholics in attendance and others who still suffer.

Teams and organizations, tribes and communities—essentially any group of human beings navigating real time together—can experience this phenomenon of dynamic attunement. All it takes is a trigger to get people moving and enough individuals tuning into and communicating what's going on inside and outside their group. Using their collective awareness as a compass, the group can initiate real-time course corrections, as necessary, that are consistent with a shared vision and purpose.

Unconscious Awareness

Awareness is another way to think about listening.

Whatever we can observe is actionable. Whatever we cannot observe is not actionable. Therefore, understanding that awareness and listening are different ways of talking about the same phenomenon allows the arena of our awareness to be more actionable.

We can change our awareness through changing our listening. And we can change our listening by making new, and often unprecedented, commitments.

Just as we can be unaware of our already listening, we can also be unaware of how our listening affects how we observe the world and, consequently, impacts our behavior. This "unconscious awareness", this capacity for our behavior to be automatic, is a powerful and positive aspect of how we normally navigate in life. In a real-time world, we need to be conscious of the background or context in which we are moving so that we don't become blind or fall into denial with respect to our blind spots. Cognitive blindness is a fact of the human condition. Being blind to our blindness is a consequence of the paradigm in which we are operating. When we know we are blind and something is not working, we can stop, inquire into the structure of our own thinking, and formulate new possibilities.

So what does it take to remain present to ourselves, others, and what is occurring—all at the same time—while we are in action?

Practice. What we practice is observing listening, generating listening, and being grounded in the moment.

Athletes and athletic teams who have many hours of practice under their belts often report that they don't think before moving into action. They sense what is happening and what is about to happen and move with it. Their body somehow seems to *know* what to do.

Professional baseball players, for example, observe that they swing at a ball that has been thrown to them before thinking. It seems to them as if a kind of instantaneous *awareness of the ball as it is being thrown* informs their body to move. Race car drivers, who are moving so fast that taking time to think would mean it's too late to make a turn, suggest that their awareness is *projected into the future*. They've learned to trust their bodies to move in a kind of harmony with how their world is occurring.

This phenomenon of "awareness without thinking" or being "in the zone" is not limited to athletes. An increasing number of people practice mindfulness techniques to discipline themselves to bring their attention to whatever is happening in the present moment and to tap into their unthinking awareness. Most of us have experienced being in the zone in emergencies, in very intimate moments with friends or lovers, or perhaps when practicing an art or hobby. And people who work in roles that require they be fully present like E.R. doctors, firefighters, and video game superstars develop and rely on this alert, unthinking wakefulness. Through practice, they have embodied the distinctions of their profession and are capable of extraordinary performance in real time.

Conscious Awareness

Data and information can satisfy our curiosity and bolster confidence in our decisions. But when they bombard us on all sides as they usually do these days, they can be overwhelming.

Busy navigators may use staff or artificial intelligence services to filter and curate the many data inputs coming at them. Having someone or something else pick and choose what is of interest to us can be useful; however, this practice can also blind us to what is outside of our thinking palette. Namely, what we don't know we don't know.

First, we usually set the parameters for sorting and responding to our various inputs based on what we *think* will be important, interesting, or valuable. Yet we cannot anticipate all the inputs we will receive in the future. The parameters we design may very well lead us into missing out on new perspectives and unforeseen circumstances that will be essential to our navigation. Second, our inputs, no matter how broad or diverse they may be, cannot represent everything that is going on in the world. We need to be consciously aware that what is missing will be, more often than not, a blindness and a potential threat to what we are trying to achieve.

This reveals another paradoxical challenge of navigating in real time. We are relating to and sorting through all the various conversations and information we encounter on a daily basis, while simultaneously organizing our choices around the specific vision or intention on which we are focused.

Struggling to balance input with intention often shows up as stress in our bodies. If we think of ourselves as fixed entities, we often begin to collapse into a mood of overwhelm as soon as we sense our "glass is full". We can go into cognitive overload, shut down, and become closed to anything new.

If we can remain curious and not try to control our "input", then everything can be of interest. We can take in new input or leave it, moment to moment, and appropriate just what we need in a given situation. We can share inquiry into a new topic or area of concern with others, start to make sense of it, and learn together.

When we relate to input as something to be selectively appropriated, we can stay open and present, grounded in our journey and our purpose or intention in such a way that new and unexpected ideas and information come *to us* with opportunities. We can start to see anomalies in our world and relate to them as signs of emerging possibilities and new pathways, new norms and practices that can become embedded in our culture and our bodies.

Being open and present is a learned practice, a practice that includes being in action. One that embraces both sensing what is in the wider landscape and focusing on the task at hand. A jet pilot, for example, is situationally aware, taking in multiple inputs from the environment, the aircraft, the crew, and the air traffic controllers, while still being 100% present and focused on landing the plane.

To a large extent, when we are open and present, both our conscious and unconscious awarenesses naturally come into play.

Moods

Human beings—all of us—are always in some mood or another, whether positive or negative. Unlike emotions (which tend to be very specific and relatively short-lived), moods are like the background music playing in the movie of our life. This constant "mood track" does not cause our experience or our behavior, but is always correlated with our listening and adds a whole range and depth to our experience of living.

Listening to our moods is like listening to the soundtrack of a film. Sometimes we are aware of the tune. Other times, all we hear are the sounds of silence. Usually we have a story about why we are in a particular mood, which tends to reinforce the mood. Other times, we justify our moods by blaming—our circumstances, other people, our relationships, our past, even the weather. Nevertheless, our moods are always there, subtly (and sometimes not so subtly) influencing how we relate to what is happening.

In the normal course of living, our moods can shift rapidly from one to another, depending on how we are relating to the world and our circumstances. Circumstances change in our life's movie: there's a plot twist. Suddenly, our buttons get pushed and a mood gets triggered. In a bad mood, nothing seems to be going our way. In a good mood, it can seem as if nothing can go wrong. Our biology responds sympathetically: our energy levels can tumble or soar, our appetite decreases or increases, we smile or mope around.

Moods often seem to come and go without warning, almost as if they are happening *to* us.

Windows

Navigating the world is a matter of paying attention to both the content and the context of life. All too often, we focus exclusively on the content and miss the context.

The body acts as our window on the world. Biological phenomena, very specific and noticeable, happen as our real-time responses to objects, people, and events. For example, we will very likely notice our heart rate accelerate and our muscles stiffen when someone brandishes a gun in our face and yells, "Hands up!". We may observe the knot in the pit of our stomach and the tension in our neck and shoulders as we intensely focus on brainstorming with colleagues, trying to solve an urgent problem with little to no resources. Or we may sense a smile creeping across our face and warmth around our heart as a toddler shares something they've just discovered. All of these physical sensations can actually point us to the context of that moment.

Moods are a context within which we relate to our world. As context, moods influence and limit our possibilities. For example, when we're in a mood of fear or doubt, almost anything in our circumstances can appear to threaten our future. When we're in a mood of enthusiasm or joy, any situation may appear as a possibility.

Many of us believe that our moods are caused by whatever is going on in our world. I disagree: I believe that our moods shape how what is going on occurs for us, which in turn impacts our choices, our actions, and our results. As historical phenomena, moods actually disclose the lingering subtle narratives that help us "tune" ourselves to the situations of our lives. As author Gloria Flores so aptly put it, *"Moods are windows to our assessments and to the standards that support them."*[6] It takes some skill to recognize them, to consciously use them to orient ourselves in our world, and to discern the connection between our moods and our situations.

Interpretations

Most of us believe our moods are psychological in nature. After all, most of us experience a mood as a feeling or as something personal that happens inside our mind or body.

From my perspective, moods are historical in nature. That is, they occur when what's happening is consistent or inconsistent with our historical interpretation—our story—of the world. When something occurs that matches or even exceeds our expectations, it will naturally pull for a mood of **acceptance**. When something occurs that doesn't match our narrative, it will pull for a mood of **resistance**. This generally takes the form of an unfulfilled expectation or a view that reality should be different from what it is. No matter what is occurring or when, our choice in every moment is to either accept or resist, which in turn will influence our moods.

There are many labels we can use to describe our moods. In general, they correspond with this choice of resistance or acceptance and with our orientation to time. Resisting the past, for instance, will generally trigger some form of resentment; resisting what is happening in the moment may trigger resignation; resisting something about the future may provoke anxiety or fear. Conversely, when we accept the past as simply a story and "what is" as it is, we will naturally experience some peace of mind or serenity. When we accept what is happening now, we are focused and engaged. When we accept a future possibility, we can experience moods of ambition, hope, and passion.

Moods of Acceptance/Resistance in Time[7]

	PAST	PRESENT	FUTURE
ACCEPT	Serenity	Engagement	Ambition
RESIST	Resentment	Resignation	Anxiety

We don't always notice that there is always an accompanying story associated with each of our moods. For example, the mood of resentment is some variation of a "you wronged me before and will do it again" story that has our sympathetic nervous system generate tension in resistance to whatever it is we are supposedly resenting. In a mood of resignation, we have a story that there is no possibility, a story that initiates the collapse of our bodies inwards. That story, after all, means there is no possibility, which justifies giving up on whatever we've become resigned about. The mood of ambition comes with the exact opposite story—there is possibility—which stirs our sympathetic nervous system to pump up our bodies.

The story often includes an explanation for why we've been triggered, but it is not the cause of the mood. Explanations are never the action. The action is to separate our story from our mood. In doing so, we alter our relationship with the mood and, in most cases, will have a choice about how we respond.

Influences

Moods are never just personal to an individual. Moods always occur as social phenomena. And they can be contagious.

We can observe and be caught up in other people's moods—just as we can infect others with our moods. Who hasn't been sucked into the discomfort of the blues or the doldrums at one time or another? Who hasn't also found themselves resisting someone else's mood and then— without wanting to—falling themselves into a bad mood about the other person's mood? When a bad mood prevails for the majority of the people in a group, that mood can suffuse the whole group. Fortunately, we've also seen these moods quickly disappear in the presence of someone else's stronger mood.

In addition to the fleeting day-to-day moods we have, we can also distinguish deeper and more pervasive moods that live in our cultural conversations. These collective moods inform our core attitudes and ways of being. Almost semi-permanent, often grounded in our culture's stories about life and the world, they influence how we experience our lives. Collective moods occur as cultural phenomena and reflect the relationships we have with ourselves and our circumstances.

Today, for example, many people in the developed world live in a mood of more or less constant anxiety, afraid of losing their job, reinforced by a story they have about their financial situation. They look at what has happened historically to people in similar circumstances in their culture and then expect the same for themselves. Yet, we can observe many impoverished people elsewhere in the world who are *not* experiencing anxiety. There is, therefore, no cause-and-effect relationship between one's financial situation and one's mood. The story and the cultural expectations these fearful individuals have about what is required for happiness—not the size of their pay check—are the source of their anxiety.

Moods occur as shared spaces within which groups and even societies relate to the world. Most societies evolve within certain deep moods and attitudes toward life and the world. These patterns of collective mood tend to persist for long periods and typically are lumped under the explanation, "That's the way we are." For example, certain Latin and Mediterranean cultures are characterized by a very sensual and joyous connection with life: that mood can be present and dominant even when an individual within that culture is having a bad day. Other cultures may be characterized as more reserved or more melancholy.

Another common and destructive mood is resignation, the mood we experience when we believe we have no power to change our circumstances and no possibility. In some countries that have paternalistic, highly authoritarian cultures, it is not unusual or surprising to find a majority of the population living in a story of "no possibility" and a state of powerlessness. Their mantra: "That's just the way it is, so why bother trying to do anything about it?" Citizens may become so resigned that they don't even question authority, let alone generate organized ways of changing the story or the culture. On the other hand, there are countries with similar circumstances in which the citizens have created broadly shared moods of serenity and acceptance as a cultural context for their way of living.

Present & Committed

When we engage in lengthy explanations of why we're feeling the way we feel or why we are in one mood or another, we are typically focused on the past. When we continuously give uncommitted opinions about the world, our situation, or why something can't be done, we are reinforcing the prevailing story we have about the future. Time spent talking about these things can, in effect, pull us away from the urgency of the moment and trap us in historical conversations that do not add any value to what we want to accomplish. They have us become spectators of life, removed from actions that might alter the future. When life is moving very fast, we simply don't have time for these conversations.

While there may be some cathartic value in sharing our mood and its accompanying story with others, doing so rarely changes anything. Enrolling others and gaining their agreement with our story only justifies the mood and adds to its persistence. We no longer have the time to indulge our moods the way we did in the slower, more stable environments of the past. Today, we are learning instead to separate our moods from our stories.

Who you are is not your mood.

Many of our negative moods are connected to our expectations and beliefs about what people or our circumstances should be, but often are not. Indulging our mood/stories traps us in the "victim" role. That role, combined with a need to understand and have certainty in a rapidly changing world, produces more stress, more anxiety, and more negative moods, all of which further reinforces our victimhood. Truly a vicious cycle.

How to escape?

How can we be present to our moods and shift them to ones more supportive of the future we want to create?

We can focus on two things:

- The present moment (rather than the past or future), and
- Our commitments (rather than our stories).

This is what we have historically counted on our surgeons, pilots, and police to do in a crisis. When a great deal is at stake and time is of the essence, we expect them to stay focused on what is needed right now. We rely on them to be clear and in action on their commitment to our health and safety. We expect them to put their moods aside. And if they can't, we expect them to decline to participate in whatever activity they are responsible for until they can be 100% focused on whatever the situation requires to produce a successful outcome.

This kind of clarity and commitment is now becoming an important practice for everyone all the time. Being "in a mood" can be counter-productive when used as an excuse or explanation for sub-par performance. We have to be responsible and conscious. Any disconnect from the present while surfing through real time will inevitably lead to an immediate fall or an abrupt wake-up call. Any disconnect from the present will lead to some form of reminder to focus and pay attention—or else be ready for the consequences for failing to do so.

Interestingly, moods do not generally persist when we are in action, partly because the stories that carry them become largely irrelevant and partly because our awareness is not focused on our mood when we are in action. In most cases, when we come back later to rehash how we were feeling before we moved into action, the mood has simply disappeared.

Space & Time

The ability to sense and discern moods will likely be the most intimate, sensitive listening skill we need to cultivate for navigating in real time. It requires we be fully present to observe context, how we are being, and what's between people in each moment—without getting distracted by our expectations and without getting addicted to the content of our circumstances. Shifting how the world occurs for ourselves and how it occurs for others will create space for different moods to arise. Moods more conducive to creating contexts for learning, collaboration, and innovation. Moods more suited to sensing how we can take care of what we care about and create a world that works.

Our biggest challenge will be the fact that moods move through space and time with us, wherever we go, until they dissipate. Temporal and transportable, they connect our past, present, and future. Our mood generally corresponds to the story we are living, the story we have about how we are, how we perceive the world, and how we believe things should or should not be. In this way, moods take things that are generally rooted in the past, like preexisting interpretations, and project them into the future as predictions and expectations. They also expose what we are thinking about what our current reality should be, or increasingly, what it could be. If we expect something good to be happening and it isn't, we might get upset, frustrated, or dejected. If something good is happening that we didn't expect, we might be pleasantly surprised and happy.

Being also contagious, moods tend to color our relationships with everyone and everything. The upset we have in one situation or relationship quietly spills over into others without our noticing. That recurring frustration with early morning traffic spills over into our first meeting of the day and persists like a bad habit. That unresolved issue with our parents has us become, yet again, tense and defensive when we're talking to our boss.

Ever-Changing

Can we learn to recognize and manage moods? Can we generate positive moods such as joy, confidence, and satisfaction—even in the most uncertain times and potentially difficult circumstances? I believe we can.

Rarely do we choose our moods. We do, however, have a choice about how we relate to each one as we become aware of it.

We can resist it. That is, we can fail to accept it. In which case, we become prisoners of the mood. The mood literally "has" us.

Or we can choose the mood we are in. That is, we can fully accept it. We can recognize and accept what we have done that contributes to our mood. We can accept the mood *and* the story that came with it. In doing so, we free ourselves from being owned by both.

Learning to do this is a matter of: 1) observing moods as phenomena, 2) practicing accepting them (rather than resisting them), and 3) consciously choosing what we listen for. For instance, if something happens and my mood shifts from serene to angry, I can learn to acknowledge the anger without getting caught up in the story and blaming whatever I might consider to be the cause of my anger. The better I get at observing my moods as they shift without being swept away in drama and blame, the more I can include each mood as a part of my experience without it dominating and controlling my responses and my relationships with others.

If we understand listening as the background interpretation that is organizing our relationship with what is occurring in our lives, we can also understand our moods as a manifestation of our "already listening". If my already listening is that you cannot be trusted, then my mood will be defensive or guarded whenever I enter a conversation with you. If I notice that my mood is shifting to anger as we talk, I can **choose to listen for** commitment or for possibility to shift my mood again to something more positive, like curiosity or openness.

Interestingly, when we are really present in the moment, our moods are either transparent or irrelevant. When we experience the past, present, and future as one whole, there is no need to re-act.

For everything is action. Knowing this is the key to being able to navigate in a real-time world.

Chapter 5

COMMUNICATING:
the art of relating

Relating and communicating are heads and tails of the same coin: they are the currency for change and accomplishment.

Why Relating?

We exist in an ocean of relationship.

For many of us, our relationships are so ubiquitous that much of the time we are not even aware that our reality is a relational phenomenon. This blindness can have us trapped in our individuality and imagining we are separate from others and the world.

Yet I, as an individual, can only exist in relationship with others. Everything that I can imagine or experience occurs in my relationship with something or someone else.

Language allows us to distinguish between something or someone and our relationship with that person or thing. Language allows us to think abstractly and imagine relationships that don't exist. Even our thinking is constituted by dichotomy (a relationship between two things): we can't think "up" without "down", "near" without "far". Language also allows us to speak *about* "relationship" as a concept. Even this, in itself, requires that we have a relationship between ourselves as an observer and what is being observed.

We are constantly in some form of conversation either with ourselves or others. We are always speaking and listening—with the exception of those transcendental moments when we are so totally present in meditation or in action that our self-awareness disappears. We are not only in conversations about what is happening, but we are also creating and reinforcing our reality and our relationship with our reality through conversations.[1]

As we communicate in conversation, we are creating or recreating our relationships within our world. Likewise, when we change how we relate with something or someone, it alters our conversations as well. We can more easily see in real time that the distinction between relationship and communication is not only blurred but, for all intents and purposes, it disappears in the moment. Relationship and communication become two aspects of a "whole", like heads and tails of a coin.

Relationship and communication are the access to action when navigating.

In a real-time world, authority has less and less power. There is little to no time for order giving and taking. We have to trust each other implicitly, count on each other for different things, and be responsible for the success and well-being of the whole. On a world-class team, for example, we move seamlessly together as one, using conversations to forward all of the action.

Several things (besides technology) make it possible for people to operate as a synchronized team, to be very present and connected with each other, moving as one, no matter what is going on. These include a shared purpose to which we are all committed. Being personally responsible for what is occurring, including the future. Clear, committed communications. Recognition that we are all co-creating the future, all the time. And relationships with each other, our circumstances, and time that are appropriate to what's unfolding.

When we find ourselves in a natural disaster like a hurricane, an earthquake, or a flood, we, more often than not, witness people coming together to coordinate a response. Certainly some people panic; they resist the circumstances and refuse to participate. Others opt out, either because of disability or illness, from participating; they are the most at risk of further hurt. Everyone else is on deck, present with their shared circumstances, focused on doing what needs to be done. For these people, a kind of spontaneous relatedness emerges; they feel they naturally belong to a "team" and focus their communications on what they're committed to taking care of. The superfluous typically disappears. Collective moods of care and support, gratitude and appreciation generally appear. These situations often stand out as the most memorable in our lives and become the standard by which we measure whether we are being the best we can be.

Cultivating our capacity for relationship and our capacity for generating conversation allows us to navigate in a world in which both relationship and communication are always present and available. We might say that relating and communicating are the means by which life as we know it is possible. They are what we are always doing when navigating real time.

We have talked in previous chapters about navigators learning to listen powerfully to become increasingly present to what is occurring. We have also talked about navigators needing to learn to distinguish moods—their own and those of others—as the first step in being able to generate conversations that can shift those moods to be more consistent with or appropriate to what people are trying to accomplish. This first step of discernment will involve articulating the numerous subtle expressions of mood, rather than relying on simple generalizations of "good" or "bad", "positive" or "negative".

Moods are not inherently positive nor negative. It is our relationship to them which makes them positive or negative.

If I am impatient when I need to be calm in a particular situation, then the impatience becomes the context through which I listen to others and through which others listen to me. The impression I create of not caring about their concerns will impact the results I can achieve with them. Labelling the impatience "negative", in this case, could be deemed appropriate; however, we want to watch out for the tendency to use a "negative" mood as an excuse for anything less than stellar results.

We as navigators realize that ignorance of people's moods and commitments, including our own, jeopardizes our ability to navigate effectively through a real-time world. We can, after all, use moods as openings for connection and conversation, alignment and coordination. And so becoming more aware of and responsible for our relationships makes sense. Ideally, as we begin to discern the narratives that have certain moods persist, we will listen to ourselves and others with a greater depth of understanding and compassion.

Always Already Related

We are all autonomous—yet interdependent—human beings. We are always already related to each other, always already connected with everyone else on the planet. And yet, quite often we're not really present to our fundamental relatedness.

Our relationships are central to our happiness, our identity, our value, our accomplishments. When things happen around us that we don't expect or don't think should happen, we often find ourselves feeling disconnected or incomplete. What we almost always do is blame someone, which undermines our relationship with that person or group. So we look for a relationship with someone else—a partner, a friend, a guru, a community—to alleviate our discomfort. In doing so, we are living into a story that we are "not enough", "not connected" or "not belonging" to this group, this situation, this world. But that is just a narrative, not the truth.

We have a choice. We can let that story run us. Or we can resist it and try to get connected (which only ensures the persistence of the story). Or we can acknowledge we have a story that says we are not connected and use it to help us focus on being present. We can facilitate presence through engagement and inquiry. Knowing we are always already connected, we can simply pay attention to others as we move through the world.

We can choose to be curious.

Who is this other person in front of us?
What is happening with them?
How do we want to relate to them?
Do we trust them? Fear them? Love them?
Do we want to collaborate with them in this situation?
Make a commitment to them?
What conversation do we want to have with them?

Curiosity gives us the possibility of creating every moment in every relationship as an original.

We pay handsomely to see great actors who can perform the same star role in the same stage production, night after night, show after show, year after year. Actor Rex Harrison played the part of Henry Higgins in the hit musical *My Fair Lady* for two solid years in New York and another year in London. He wrote that, "...after a long run the part becomes so automatic that if you falter you forget everything, and you simply can't go on.... If you've done it [the play] eight times a week for a year, or two years, your mind is apt to wander a little bit, and if it wanders for a second and you think; what am I going to have for supper? in the middle of it all, you don't know where you are for a minute, then you catch it again. But it gives you such a mental shock that for a week you're terrified it's going to happen again."[2] Dame Maggie Smith alluded to Rex's ability to remain present with his fellow actors and make every moment of every performance an original at his memorial in 1990: "He gave every line, every *thought*, a freshness—an elusive immediacy that every actor would love to possess."[3]

We all have this capacity to create every moment as an original.

Commitment

Whatever definition we use, the phenomenon of commitment is central to our species. The ability to commit and then act upon a commitment, a competency that begins in language and that distinguishes us from other animals, may be constitutive of what it means to be a human being.

Some interpret the word "commitment" to mean a duty. Several dictionaries define the word as a "state of being". For twentieth-century French philosopher Sartre, it has the quality of "emotional and moral engagement". For many, it means an obligation. For still others, the word suggests the source of our self-expression and the possibility of choice. I think of commitment as an action—an action in language—that usually occurs in conversation. An action that gives us access to and power in relationships with others.

We often offer words like "bold", "courageous", or "confident" to explain why one person commits and another does not.

Our commitments are the flow of life. We don't necessarily think about "commitment" when we arrange to meet a friend for coffee, make a doctor's appointment, or tell our daughter we'll pick her up from school. But that is what they are. These everyday commitments to action are part of growing up and living within the norms of a particular culture. Actually, for most of human history, the action of committing has been a foundation of human society and civilization.

We cannot take commitment for granted in a real-time world. Committing is a way of orienting ourselves when we don't have maps and we don't know where we are going. If we don't use our commitments to navigate, then we will keep bouncing around all over the place or we'll get stuck circling in a vicious cycle.

As navigators, our job is not to focus on the outcomes of particular commitments. It is primarily to know where we are relative to where we came from and relative to our commitments. Let's say we commit to traveling east on foot for three days. We may not know our final destination or how to get there. But we do know where we are relative to where we started and relative to our commitment to travel east.

Commitment is an essential aspect of human coordination and to living in community. Most can agree that we live our lives in networks of relationships and that we're always communicating in one way or another. Navigating in a real-time world necessitates we coordinate our actions with clarity and efficiency. In the "now", we want to make choices based on what we or others are committed to, recognizing that the fulfillment or lack of fulfillment of these commitments will impact our identity in the world as being reliable or trustworthy and, as a consequence, will affect our relationships with others.

If we view communication competencies as essentially being about expressing and assessing our commitments, then we can appreciate that every conversation will have consequences—on our relationship with ourselves and our relationships with others.

Every relationship is an opportunity to remain present to and be responsible for our commitments in the moment.

Trust

We are always committed.

We find commitments in every instance of human creation and coordination. Commitments that may have been spoken in words (such as "I promise"). Commitments that may have been expressed non-verbally and that speak louder than words (such as a nod, a handshake, or a signature). Commitments that allow us to create a possibility, a vision, or a dream and then mobilize our relationships and our conversations to realize that future.

In 1980, Fernando Flores wrote that commitments can occur in different domains and have different impacts.[1]

- A request, an offer, or a promise is a commitment to action
- A declaration is a commitment to "the way it is" or "what will be"
- Assessments and assertions are commitments to some understanding or viewpoint about what is occurring, what has occurred or what might occur—but only to the extent people are committed to the way they see the world and are responsible for their

judgements (otherwise, their views are pure opinion without commitment to any specific possibility or action).

Where do our commitments come from?

I believe that commitment emerges from our relationships.

We generate commitments when we experience an opening, when we observe something is missing, or when we are simply motivated by what we imagine might be. Someone asks us to go out on a date—and we pause before choosing whether to accept. Our boss requests that we take on an urgent project to produce a particular outcome at work—and we pause again before choosing whether to take on the extra work. Someone mentions a way to take care of something we care about that no one else is doing yet—and we pause and reflect on what might be if we choose to start a new enterprise.

A choice is a commitment. And a commitment is a social phenomenon involving a speaker and a listener— even when we commit to ourselves.

If the listener takes the commitment seriously, then they will respond accordingly. In this case, we can say that the person is a "committed listener". A committed listener will typically call a person to account if they make a promise and don't keep it or, in some cases, will assist the committed person to fulfill their commitment.

If the listener does not take the commitment seriously, they will maintain a "we shall see" or "prove it to me" posture. Because the "uncommitted listener" has no stake in the commitment, they have no responsibility for whether the commitment is realized or not.

Commitments to ourselves very often fall into this latter category: they are weak and more like wishes (think New Year's Resolutions). That is, unless we enlist a support group or surrender to something larger than ourselves to enable us to distinguish that part of ourselves that commits (the observer) and the automatic rationalizing part of ourselves that explains away and justifies why we cannot or do not keep our commitments.

The majority of our commitments are made to another person or persons. Responsibly holding ourselves to account for our choices and our actions in the context of our commitments is an integral part of our relationships. If I'm in a relationship and something happens that puts my commitment to the other person(s) at risk of not being fulfilled, I can communicate what is happening to whomever I made the commitment to and either revoke, renegotiate, or modify the commitment *unless new ideas and resources can be brought to bear to keep my original commitment.*

People who live committed lives, who "walk their talk" and act responsibly in this way, have identities within their communities as individuals who are trustworthy. They are generally more accomplished and/or successful than those who avoid or consistently qualify their commitments with, "I will do it *if...*". When people don't keep their commitments (even when they have a good reason) and don't communicate with the people impacted by this, trust erodes.

"Between stimulus and response there is a space.
In that space is our power to choose our response.
In our response lies our growth and our freedom."
Viktor E. Frankl[4]

Authenticity

How do we know if someone is committed?

Commitments are actions in language. If someone says they are committed and we assume they are sincere and competent to make that commitment, then we should take them at their word *even if they fail to keep the commitment.* If they repeatedly fail to keep their commitment, we may question their competence or challenge their practices for communicating. But neither incompetence nor poor communications mean the person was not committed.

When we assess that someone's failure to fulfill a commitment is evidence that they were not committed, we are actually accusing the person of lacking sincerity. This is a very serious breach of trust and the damage to the relationship can be quite difficult to overcome. My assumption will always be that a person is sincere and authentic in making their commitments until they either repeatedly fail to keep their word, show no responsibility for not doing so, or neglect to acknowledge their own ignorance or lack of competence in a specific area.

When trust is lost, I believe it is also important to communicate this to the person with as much specificity as possible. Being specific, you could say to the person who agrees to meet you for lunch, consistently does not show up, and doesn't offer any regret or responsibility for doing so, "I no longer trust you to keep a social date with me." That doesn't necessarily mean I don't trust them when it comes to delivering weekly reports to me at work on time. Too often trust is lost in a particular situation and then generalized to the entire relationship, which leaves both parties with little room to coordinate. If mistrust has indeed infected the relationship and it is an important one to you, you could rebuild it. However, reaching a state of complete forgiveness will take time and a great deal of care and rigor with regard to the keeping of new commitments.

Does this mean we have to fulfill all our commitments to be authentic and/or sincere?

No. But we have to responsible for our commitments.

If we keep *none* of our commitments, then our word is meaningless. We are unlikely to have much power in the world.

If we keep *all* of our commitments, we are essentially setting our bar low to avoid putting ourselves or our identity at risk. We limit our power.

A commitment is an action made by an individual. Each commitment made by that individual belongs to that person. That individual—and only that individual—has the power and the responsibility to revoke or renegotiate each of their commitments with the people involved as soon as they are aware they no longer want to or can fulfill them. Explanations or rationales are never the cause for not keeping a commitment.

If we don't take care to acknowledge when we are no longer committed, if we don't revoke or renegotiate and offer explanations when appropriate, then the people to whom we are making commitments will begin to stop trusting us. At some point, they will stop taking our commitments seriously.

In most cases, changing a commitment is not a serious break in relationship if the other person is given ample opportunity to adjust *their* commitments. When circumstances or our intentions change, announcing the change early is important. Waiting to announce the change in our commitment until after it is due comes across as an excuse and only increases the probability of a break in the relationship. In this case, we need to offer sincere apologies and, when appropriate, accept whatever costs may accompany the change (such as losing a deposit or incurring some debt to the other person).

Responsibility

We could, of course, turn to one of the many theories and models of relationship at this point to get at the "how" of relating. In my experience, however, these generally focus on attempting to figure out the individual characteristics or attributes that best determine the nature and quality of a relationship. I've come to appreciate that, just as there are about as many techniques and styles as there are relationships, there are countless exceptions to these lists of characteristics.

The art of relating is not about technique or style or attributes. It is about our ability to generate relationships with each other, even though we are different.

To be generative, we can declare that we are responsible for everything in our relationships, including our communications. By responsible, I mean we are "response-able". We have an ability to respond. This responsibility isn't about causality: it does not prescribe what I will or will not do in my relationships.

This notion of responsibility as a way of being is very counter-intuitive. By declaration, I can be responsible for anything at any moment. If I only relate to a person or thing responsibly when I have control, then I set limits on possibility and freedom. Choosing to relate to a person or thing responsibly *by declaration* gives me freedom to choose how I will relate to everything else that occurs— whether I have control or not.

From this perspective of owning it all, there is no limit on what I can choose to own or be responsible for. We don't choose what others do and have little or no control over what they do, but we always have a choice in how we relate to them. As long as I can hold myself responsible for all of it, I am generating my relationship.

Whatever we are not responsible for, we are a victim of.

The moment I cannot be responsible for any part of any relationship, I have defaulted to viewing that relationship as bigger than I am. As a consequence, I will blame, offer excuses, and cope with or try to change myself or the other person.

For example, if we listen closely to conversations in most organizations today, we will hear endless explanations and excuses when things are not going well. These negative conversations inevitably destroy possibility and cover up personal responsibility by those in the conversations. When I've asked people to tell me what do we say when we want to kill a possibility, the list will almost always include, "They won't approve," "We tried that...", "We can't afford it...", "We don't have enough resources...", and "It's too risky...". The list goes on and on. These kinds of conversations blind us to the fact that our conversation *itself* is causing the persistence of the status quo and trapping us in a prison of our conventional wisdom. Our complaints and justifications leave us with only having the choice of reacting to whatever we are complaining about or, at best, coping with the situation.

Perhaps the worst consequences of not being responsible occur in our interpersonal relationships. This often takes the form of what Fernando Flores has termed "cordial hypocrisy"[5] in which people maintain a pretense of trust while avoiding making commitments to each other, withholding negative assessments from each other, and not taking each other's commitments seriously. This can further lead to negative moods such as resentment and resignation, fuel gossip, and undermine who we can be for each other. What is ironic in most organizations is that, when we have negative assessments of others, we tend to relate to them based on those assessments. We don't tell them our assessments: this further erodes not only trust between us as individuals, but ultimately erodes trust in ourselves as well.

Choice & Relationship

Choice is an action. Most of us would agree it is an action that we take as individuals.

I make a distinction between freely choosing and deciding. Freely choosing is 100% created. Deciding is making a selection among available options.

For example, if you lived in one house all your life, you could rearrange your furniture within the predefined parameters of the building to change your environment. You would be deciding among *options*, not choosing from possibilities. To be choosing, you would have to realize that your "house" was simply one possibility and then create other *possibilities*. Then you could exercise your choice from among the possibilities you've invented: stay or leave, buy or build, rent or lease, join an intentional community or sell your furniture and travel the world.

I have the view that, while I make choices, I cannot make them alone.

To choose, I need to always have a context or possibility bigger than my point of view.

Without that bigger context or possibility, I will automatically default to selecting what I consider to be the best option available. To choose necessitates that we have a relationship with someone or something outside ourselves. In other words, from my perspective, I cannot observe the framework or context within which I am choosing. I cannot see any possibility bigger than my own point of view. I need the perspective of a trusted "other" to observe my framework. From this other person's perspective, I can see the framework within which I am choosing. I also have the possibility of creating a different framework.

This practice of "reframing" is a powerful tool when coaching anyone, especially leaders, to have them see their situation or challenge from a different perspective. It is even more powerful when a person can experience and embody a new perspective or possibility and move into action and develop new behaviors. While reframing is useful to provoke new thinking and sometimes innovation, it is a rational process. Insights and new concepts will amount to nothing without a concurrent commitment to action and new practices to embody what is being learned.

On Differences

Paradoxically, while it's true that we're always already related to everybody, the nature of human relationships has traditionally been oriented towards tribalism, racism, and the other "isms" that are a product of our being blind to or in denial of this fact. Just look at the social institutions we human beings have created—nation states, tribes, and classes—that reinforce our differences and keep us apart.

I remember hearing Václav Havel, former president of the Czech Republic, say in a radio interview, "In the womb, there are no differences between human beings." In a speech he gave at Stanford University in 1994, he stated, "there exist deep and fundamental experiences shared by the entire human race, and that traces of such experiences can be found in all cultures, regardless of how distant or how different they are from one another."[6]

Being able to acknowledge and transcend our differences is increasingly becoming an important part of navigating in our real-time world. The Internet and social media may facilitate this transcendence of differences—or they may not. Like most technologies, they can be used for good or for evil. It remains to be seen whether they effectively bring humanity closer together or contribute to the fragmentation and polarization that are pulling us apart.

The fact is that, in a real-time world, we can no longer afford the luxury of indulging ideological, political, cultural, or ethnic differences at the expense of others. While we can have and value and appreciate our unique traditions, we must give up the need or belief that others must agree with us. We are living in increasingly pluralistic situations where we need to recognize and respect our differences, as well as our similarities. In this world, the best leaders are those who can stand in other people's shoes and create ways to align and coordinate differences, rather than exert pressure to have everyone agree with each other.

Historically, the best of politics has been the art of compromise. In a real-time world, the best of politics will be creating larger contexts, larger possibilities, that can include everyone and using conflict and differences to provoke dialogue. Those who insist on holding onto a single worldview and attempting to bludgeon others into agreement will simply be left behind and, should they be in positions of power, will become increasingly isolated or bankrupt in the futile attempt to maintain a semblance of permanence in an impermanent, real-time world.

How We Relate

In some cultures, the common sense view of relationship is that we relate for a particular purpose. In other cultures, they just relate for the sake of relating. When we are talking about competency in relating in the context of real time, we are talking about the ability to build powerful relationships and to relate appropriately connected to whatever we are trying to accomplish.

While we value our relationships, we rarely think of *how we relate* as a competency.

Even when we assess the social skills of ourselves and others in terms of how "good" we are with people, we are generally looking at techniques for "getting along". When life is moving slowly in a more or less stable world, we can apply what we learned in the past about getting along to the present almost without thinking. However, in a world of accelerating change, lack of control, unpredictability, and increasing complexity, we can no longer rely on our past experiences, our assumptions, and our expectations in relationships to guide us. We also no longer have the luxury of time to indulge in long and often tedious circular reasoning to understand why we or other people do what we do or why a situation is the way it is. That illusion of control over what happens in the future has been shattered.

Most of the time we take our relationships for granted, rarely reflecting on them. Some relationships exist by virtue of mere proximity, like being members of the same graduating class. Others are loose associations, such as the shared identity we have with all people in our profession. And then there are what I call conscious or intentional relationships.

Our relationships with other people are typically a function of our affinity and common interests. Even family relationships, while givens, are organized around whatever stories we have from our past about each other and ourselves. In other words, the basis for how we relate to each other occurs in a historical context: our behaviors and actions in relationships are generally an extension of our stories and beliefs about those relationships.

We usually don't think about the context of a relationship or how we are relating to another person until we realize something isn't working and we have a problem. It's then we have an opportunity to generate the relationship in the present.

The competency of relating is, essentially, the ability to make and keep a promise. The ability to trust each other.

Consider how often we make a commitment to someone, do not fulfill it, and do not communicate with the person involved that we will not be fulfilling it. Trust is eroded or destroyed: there is a breakdown in the relationship. We get caught up in the story and the mood associated with the breakdown. We react.

Although we would like to have the relationship improve, we don't think of the ability to improve it as a skill. We live at the effect of the broken relationship for years, we run away from it, or we let it disappear from our lives entirely.

In a real-time world, we need to be able to skillfully restore respect and trust.

Speaking & Listening

Although almost everyone will agree that relationships are important, few of us look deeply into the nature of "relationship" or observe it as a phenomenon. Relationship is something so central and basic to our existence and who we are that it is generally transparent, taken as a given, or taken for granted.

We cannot observe a relationship as an object: it is not a thing. What we *can* observe is our speaking and our listening. We can observe our conversations.

The distinctions of relationship and communication are different facets of a whole, like the front and back of your hand. One cannot be without the other. We can improve our relationships by improving communication, and we can improve our communication by improving our relationships. Both communication and relationship are domains of action.

Most of us think communication is about sending and receiving messages and information. That the point of communicating is to get agreement or buy-in and elicit the "right" answer or understanding of whatever we're communicating about.

By communication, I mean everything ranging from everyday conversation and eloquent oratory to body language and "presence". Listening and speaking are all that is occurring.

As we discussed in the previous chapter, listening is the opening or context that determines how our reality occurs for us. Generating listening can alter how we relate to our circumstances and everything in our environment. It can also transform how we experience our relationships, as well as open possibilities for creating new and powerful relationships consistent with whatever we are trying to accomplish. Yes, there will need to be a sufficient background of relatedness, a common vision and some coordination of action, but all of these come about through listening and speaking in the broadest sense.

The old adage "who you are speaks so loudly that I can't hear what you're saying" points to something we've all experienced. Who a person is—their way of being—speaks. We are always expressing how we see the world, our identities, and our moods, while coordinating our commitments in the process of trying to accomplish something we can't accomplish on our own. The essence of communication, therefore, occurs in the background as a function of our context and our "ground of being" (that is, where we are coming from and our embodied interpretation of the world).

I can't observe "relationship". But I can observe my communication *about* a relationship and also my communication *in* a relationship.

If a change in a relationship is needed or wanted, the only access we have to changing it is through our communication. When we change the conversation (either the internal conversation we have with ourselves or the external conversation we have with the other person), we change the relationship. If we want to transform a problematic relationship into an authentically comfortable one, we can start a conversation to intentionally make a difference in its quality.

Communication as Dialogue

It is relatively easy to communicate and co-create relationships, possibilities, and opportunities with people who are like us. There is an almost automatic listening of each other that goes on, a sharing of a common historical narrative that acts like a conspiracy for sameness and that makes dialogue easy.

Listening only to those who share our traditions puts us at risk of developing almost unthinking co-creations.

It takes more work to connect with people who are not like us.

In a real-time world, learning how to effectively communicate and relate with people who are *not* like us is an essential navigational competency. The key to trust, collaboration, and co-creation is "dialogic" communication—communication as dialogue that leaves us with a bit more possibility than when the conversation started.

Participating in an effective dialogue requires several skills. The ability to be direct and authentic known as straight talk. The ability to listen generously, suspending judgment, and to respect and trust the other person. The ability to build the conversation, to avoid being argumentative and to remain conscious of the purpose and intent behind the dialogue. And, importantly, the willingness to offer ideas that are not yet fully formulated and to acknowledge when possibility seems to be exhausted. Develop these skills of dialogue and we can increase the effectiveness of *all* our communications and relationships.

Our ability to generate listening warrants particular attention. Most people won't listen to you until you listen to them first. When you listen deeply and generously to others to discover their concerns, you create a natural opening for dialogue. Instead of reacting to what the other person is saying in a context of being right or wrong, instead of trying to drive them toward agreeing with your point of view, you simply are present, listening and responding to the commitments they share. From there, together, new possibilities emerge which you may not have previously been aware of and appear in the dialogue.

Chapter 6

APPROPRIATING:
the art of situational learning

Appropriating is to learn just enough—without becoming trapped by what we've already learned—to be able to choose wisely, coordinate effectively, and take action responsibly in the moment.

Why Situational Learning?

Peter Senge sparked a revolution in the 1990s with *The Fifth Discipline: The Art and Practice of the Learning Organization*, which stressed that we need to continuously challenge our mental models and develop skills for creating new ways of understanding and relating to the world.[1] Now that we are operating in real time, we will want to learn to do this for a world that doesn't exist yet. We will want to be open to continuously letting go of what was accepted and taken for granted in the past as knowledge. We will want to be prepared to unlearn what we "knew" and to connect the dots from disparate fields.

Most of us believe in the critical importance of learning. In the past, the point of learning was to personally acquire knowledge, understanding, or know-how which we could then apply to solving problems, completing tasks, or accomplishing objectives. Educational institutions mostly organized teaching practices around areas of specialization to impart and reinforce specific knowledge as the foundation for success. We had to "know" before we could commit and then act. This core assumption, like many, is one that we rarely challenge. Even today, when faced with a new possibility, many of us initially respond by asking two questions: 1) "How?", and 2) "On the basis of what authority (that is, knowledge) do we know that this is really possible?".

In our real-time world, new technologies are changing the game so quickly that we don't have time to acquire, understand, and apply what we have learned in traditional ways. The pace of change continues to accelerate; knowledge in many fields is obsolete before we even get a chance to learn it; the global proliferation of smart phones and the cloud continues to expand humanity's access to information. Our relationship to knowledge, know-how, and our learning practices are evolving accordingly. The point of learning is shifting away from the **acquisition of knowledge** toward the **development of our capacity to navigate, create, and act** in any situation in real time.

Rather than learn and then apply what we've learned, we are continuously entering into and moving in the space of new conversations in order to learn. Learning now is not just a matter of googling information and brushing up on data and definitions: it is a matter of joining a conversation that is already in progress, seeing who's involved, what topics are under discussion, and what is missing.

Consider that an increasing majority of the planet's population now has real-time access to information and tools that allow them to acquire just what they need to know to effectively contribute to commerce and meaningfully participate in life. With agricultural apps, a medium-scale freehold farmer in Zimbabwe can build a farm map, measure rainfall, calculate return on investment, and connect with advisors about livestock feeding practices, disease control, and record keeping. Through online courses, an entrepreneurial engineer in India who wants to get a basic understanding of Silicon Valley's best practices in innovation as they relate to machine learning and artificial intelligence can watch videos of some of the top instructors from the best universities in the world, dialogue with course participants, and connect with subject matter experts. With a customer relationship management tool, an Asian executive can be transferred overnight to Canada knowing who the key people working in their particular field are, what concerns them, and where relationships and trust need to be developed. They can learn enough online about the history, culture, and practices of Canadians to begin to participate appropriately in that environment on short notice.

I call this learning practice *appropriation* or "situational learning". As navigators, we focus our learning on gathering enough input from the situation and the environment to articulate a coherent interpretation of where we are and what we need to consider and be responsible for, both now and in the future. We look through a lot of disparate information to find connections to our intention or project. We take data and ideas and use them in the context in which we find ourselves, often in a different way than what they have traditionally been used for. We adapt the knowledge we have gathered to make it useful in the present. We appropriate just what we need to be able to make decisions and commitments and to have enough presence, after we decide and commit, to observe what is happening right now.

If we are to learn in real time, we will want to stay present with whatever is happening without reacting. Then we can learn by simultaneously responding and adapting.

We demonstrated this innate capability when we were children playing games. We used to have no problem creating a game—a "reality"—and making our actions consistent with whatever game we were playing. The instant the rules of the game no longer made sense to us, we would throw them away, change them, start to play the game differently, or play a different game. Collaboration happened naturally and most any conflicts we had, we'd resolve through this reframing of the game. As long as we wanted to keep playing, we'd flex based upon what was called for in the moment.

This is what founders of disruptive businesses do. They invent a new game for us to play. Tesla® is bringing us electric vehicles, lithium-ion batteries, and photovoltaic panels. Coursera provides a platform for universities to offer online courses, specializations, and degrees. Boston biotech Gingko Bioworks® uses genetic engineering to produce bacteria with industrial applications. Toronto-based BlueJ Legal gives us access to artificial intelligence and machine learning to predict legal outcomes.

The founders of these disruptors did not start out having in-depth knowledge of all the elements central to their enterprises. They were able to imagine a possibility and mobilize people who did have knowledge or were capable of creating new know-how in various areas. They were able to get these people to commit and to coordinate working together very quickly to reach customers and suppliers and build infrastructures for success. Meanwhile, established companies that were grounded in the traditional belief that they need to have a lot of knowledge about the markets, what they are going to do, and how they are going to do it before they can commit to a new game were too late to garner a lion's share of the space that disruption opens up in the marketplace. The systems and practices they built to become more "agile" may have sped up their decision making—but they were still reacting to the disruptors. They were trying to acquire knowledge about something that is being created in real time—and so they were always one step behind in the game.

We stand a better chance of thriving in the midst of a messy and chaotic world when we cultivate a different relationship with learning and knowledge. We can, essentially, live a non-reactive life. Indeed, with today's technologies, we can gather historical information, identify relevant texts, listen to key people speaking online, clarify key distinctions, and assess the relevancy of ideas in a matter of days or weeks. Team members can now share concepts, questions, and concerns with other experts from around the world and consolidate their findings in a few meetings to solve very complex problems and challenges. The process of appropriation can be continuous and coincident with everything else that is going on.

Knowledge as Commodity

"Knowledge is power."

Most of us have grown up with this prevailing belief at the center of our worldview. Our educational system is built on the idea that knowledge is the key to just about everything. Education, in general, is all about learning knowledge as a prerequisite for surviving, for earning a living, for achieving social status.

In one sense, gaining knowledge and understanding is the point for many, whether that is achieved through exploration, experimentation, or experience. Specialists gather into communal guilds and professional associations to protect the skills and knowledge they possess and typically resist any change that challenges the conventional wisdom in their field or their institution. Universities, once revered as temples of learning, function more like research factories that exist to create new knowledge and push it out into the world. We admire and value scholars and scholarship for moving us closer to "the truth".

I am not against knowledge. It can be useful and interesting. Indeed, in a stable, slow-changing world, ideas like "knowledge is power" make sense.

However, in today's real-time world, knowledge is much more accessible, much more temporary in value than it ever has been. Knowledge can become, and often is, obsolete before we learn it. Some time ago, I read that more than 90% of all human knowledge has come into existence since my daughter was born and that it is doubling every twelve months. (Some have predicted that it will soon be every 12 hours.) I don't know if this is true, but if we combine knowledge and information, 90% is a probably a conservative figure. Whatever the real percentages are, there is no doubt that the amount of knowledge and information that is freely and easily available today is overwhelming.

Knowledge is now ubiquitous. It has become a commodity.

Focus on Action

Most of us have historically related to knowledge as if it is some, more or less, "true" accounting of a particular domain of human concern. How we access, define, and relate to knowledge is becoming, of necessity, fundamentally different.

We are navigating a constantly emerging, constantly shifting ocean of change together. We navigate that change in service of what we want to accomplish. In the context of navigation, our primary concern is action. We aim to learn what we need to learn to be able to get oriented in the situations in which we find ourselves, to have relevant conversations in a particular domain together, to make informed choices, and to take action.

If we are going to make a large investment of time, money, or resources in the choices we make, we don't want to do so solely based on opinions. We want to appreciate whether the information we are looking at is, indeed, "knowledge". That requires we be clear about who we are and what we're trying to accomplish as we navigate. That we become aware of the relationships, histories, and traditions involved. That we check the sources of our information and rigorously distinguish between facts and interpretations, assessments, and opinions.

Knowledge is different from facts. Knowledge tends to be a narrative within a specific context. Facts, applicable in various contexts, can be observed and verified by an objective third party. For example, we knew about and widely shared the stories of human suffering that accompanied the widespread famine in Ethiopia in the 1980s. The United Nations acknowledged that what was occurring was a famine when certain facts had been confirmed: at least 20% of households in the area faced extreme food shortages, more than 30% of children suffered from acute malnutrition, and the death rate exceeded 2 people per 10,000 per day.

More and more of the planet's population is coming online. More and more of us are now living in a universe overflowing with information, in which many things can be presented as facts and knowledge which may—or may not—be "fake news" and which may—or may not—have actual value. Clarity about the facts of the problems we face is key to solving them. One Kenyan photojournalist, Mohamed Amin, bringing photos and the story of starving people in Ethiopia to mainstream media helped alleviate suffering on a massive scale: those "leaked" photos led to an investigation into the facts and to the massive outpouring of humanitarian aid that followed.[2]

In their 2018 book *Factfulness: Ten Reasons We're Wrong About the World—And Why Things Are Better Than You Think,* co-authors Hans Rosling, Ola Rosling and Anna Rosling Rönnlund point out that, when we follow our brains as they instinctually jump to the "overly dramatic" instead of staying focused on facts, we fall into a mood of fear.[3] And in fear, we systematically mis-interpret what we are observing, equate interpretation with fact, lose touch with our critical thinking capabilities, and end up making wrong guesses about what is happening. Rely on a single perspective—our own—and we can end up exaggerating the importance of a problem and the significance of our solution. The perspectives of experts too have their limits: no one "expert" way of looking at problems works for all problems. They are also human beings and are not immune to being influenced by their mood into ignoring or being blind to that which doesn't fit with their worldview.

Fortunately, we are adapting.

An Emerging Learning Style

Conventional styles of learning focus on knowledge acquisition. For the most part, conventional learning focuses on systematically acquiring know-how and mastering skills for the purpose of applying them to earning a living. When it comes to developing competencies, this systematic learning, which gives value and weight to understanding content, is still necessary and valuable in a real-time world. However, studying "classical" knowledge, memorizing data, and embodying practices are, in and of themselves, insufficient to the challenges we are encountering in real time.

A new style of learning is emerging. A style that is always connected to action. A style with a goal of *orientation*, rather than *understanding*.

Appropriation is about *seeing* what others are learning, as distinct from *understanding* what they are saying about what they are learning. To appropriate is to stand in another person's shoes and, rather than bring their concepts inside our already existing interpretations, see things the way they see them in order to orient ourselves. Far from being disrespectful, this "borrowing" enriches our lives and helps expand our foundation for relating to a world in which knowledge can become obsolete even before we learn it.

Appropriation as a learning style allows us to navigate real-time situations inside of our commitments, intentions, concerns, and needs. In this sense, appropriation is not an alternative to learning. It is a way of *curating* and *selecting* knowledge appropriate to our specific "now".

Appropriation allows us to be more intentional, more purposeful, more selective in our learning and to choose which interpretation we want to use to navigate in each situation. Rather than acquire knowledge, know-how, or skills, we curate various interpretations. In many cases where we are entering totally new territory, there may not even be new interpretations available yet. In other cases, the game may have changed so significantly that the interpretations we have may be wrong or counter-productive.

Instead of trying to capture and hold onto a comprehensive set of data or a standard interpretation, we follow a line of interest, connecting the dots across various sources of information, reviewing multiple commentaries, looking into reviews on the pros and cons of these particular points of view. Understanding that knowledge is impermanent and historical, we can use "classical" knowledge as a resource, rather than as a prerequisite for navigation, when needed. If we intend to open a manufacturing business in Italy, for instance, rather than reading all of *The Story of Civilization* (the entire 11 volumes of Will and Ariel Durants' history of Western civilization), we can selectively acquire just what we need to know right in this moment. We don't need to read through the entire Durant series to understand how the country has evolved as a nation and a culture over the centuries. To participate in that culture without spending a lot of time on academic "book" learning, we can, if we wish, dip into the fifth volume of the Durant series on the Italian Renaissance, go online and read commentaries about it, and read reviews of the commentaries. We can also look at statistics from the World Bank on doing business in Italy, as well as more recently published books, articles, and papers to acquire multiple other interpretations and perspectives on certain aspects of manufacturing businesses in Italy. We can appreciate the "big" questions that the experts and scholars have asked and are still asking about the influence of Italy's biggest business, the mafia, on the nation's economy.

All this to discover what we might learn from the past and the present that is both appropriate and relevant to whatever it is we are navigating today.

Relevance

When we are navigating change, knowledge solely for the sake of knowledge, while it can still be intellectually satisfying, basically becomes a pastime. Independent of action, knowledge is disconnected from our real-time context and, therefore, devoid of immediate relevance.

"Knowing" what is worth knowing is a function of commitment and action. The evidence that we have acquired or appropriated worthwhile knowledge is action that moves our commitments forward. Therefore, we want to develop our capability to scope out what in the world we want to look at, scan it, skim it, and share what is relevant to what we are trying to accomplish in real time with our fellow travelers as we move forward together.

Scoping is a matter of clarifying the boundaries of our inquiry, our intentions, and our timeline. For example, what you will scope out to learn before going to work in a foreign country will be different from what you will scope out to learn before visiting the same country as a tourist.

Scanning is a matter of searching online to get a broad overview, including basic facts, of the topic of our inquiry and to prepare a short list of materials to read, listen to, and view. Through Wikipedia's bibliographic references, aggregator sites, and libraries, we can identify readily available sources of more information. We can determine who the top thought leaders in the field are, as well as competitive schools of thought or companies. We can seek out the current controversies, challenges, and predominant communities or associations.

Skimming is a matter of grazing on our short list of materials to get a sense of the fundamental ideas, distinctions, and key conversations. The point of skimming is *not* to become an expert on the topic, but to develop a sense and a sensibility for it. This process may reveal some of our own prejudices and blindspots.

Participating is a matter of hanging out where people who are interested in our topic gather, interacting in relevant conversations, and contributing what we are learning from the point of view of a beginner. Lectures, conferences, book clubs, online forums, meetups: these all offer opportunities to listen to others' ideas, opinions, and suggestions about who to speak with and what to read to further expand our understanding.

Reality Doesn't Care

An obsession with knowledge makes sense when you hold the view that the world is objective. After all, success in an objective world depends on possessing the *right* understanding of reality, having the *right* model of how the world works, and on applying this *right* knowledge to accomplishing your ambition (whatever it may be) so that you can control and predict the future.

This bias against being wrong is evident when we consider how much of our time is spent disagreeing about someone's point of view or ideas. We may arrive at some agreement through dialectic conversations. However, in the process, we all too often lose sight of the fact that agreement can come at the price of curiosity, diversity, and a creative response. In many cases, the fluidity of life's emerging reality passes us by while we are being spectators, arguing for and being trapped in points of view *which may no longer be relevant.*

Does it really matter whether we agree or disagree with a particular point of view or assessment when many of our systems, as well as the beliefs, assumptions, and conventional wisdom underlying them, are breaking down? When things are changing fast, the knowledge we learn and the understanding we have may just as quickly become obsolete. Not only that: it may very well be *wrong*. In 1977, Ken Olsen, founder of Digital Equipment, was quoted as having said, "There is no reason anyone would want a computer in their home."[4] Eighteen years later, Robert Metcalfe, co-inventor of the Ethernet and founder of 3Com, was caught on record as saying, "I predict the Internet will soon go spectacularly supernova and in 1996 catastrophically collapse."[5] In 2012, Steve Ballmer, CEO of Microsoft, said in an interview with *USA Today*, "There's no chance that the iPhone is going to get any significant market share. No chance."[6] How many businesses have missed opportunities or gone under because their leaders thought they knew something that was simply *no longer right*?

Knowledge and understanding are consolation prizes in real time: there is always a risk of getting trapped in what we have learned and understood. Our worldview is made up of many **assessments**, most of which are historical. As Fernando Flores explains, assessments "can never be directly witnessed." They are "verdicts", "declarations of what kinds of possibilities for action are open and closed to us in the future". Assessments in a particular domain of concern can be "grounded" with a collection of assertions, the number and kind of which have been agreed upon by the person making the assessment and the person hearing it, that point to a pattern in the past. On the other hand, an **assertion** "provides the hearer with something they need to take further action" and, therefore, "must involve a recognized distinction, a past action or an event that is potentially observable by anyone."[7]

However much we may want our assessments to be facts, they are still just interpretations. And as such, they are neither true nor false, neither right nor wrong.

Yet reality doesn't care what we think or feel. It just keeps occurring.

Being attached to our assessments (whether they are grounded or not) and believing in them not only shapes our mood. That attachment may also make us cognitively blind.

Behind or underlying our moods there are always assessments, some point of view we have about the situation or the world that is generally connected to our past. Our moods-assessments are the background contexts that allow us to make sense of, justify, and give meaning to our lives.

A psychologist friend was telling me of a patient of his that was in a constant mood of anxiety. When he learned that she had been in 26 automobile accidents, he asked what she had learned from all those experiences. She replied that she had learned (that is, she had an assessment) that the world is a very dangerous place. After some conversation, she could see that her assessment about the world was not true or false and she opened up to seeing other possibilities. Once she saw her blindspot, she then had the insight that *she* was the one who was dangerous. She was able to connect her recurring mood of anxiety to her story and, in doing so, let go of it. Moreover, in taking responsibility for her point of view as being neither true nor false, she was able to transform her relationship to her moods as they occurred and to have much more possibility and many more positive moods in the future.

Every Problem Is a Solution

For most of human history, the creation, acquisition, and application of knowledge has been a central aspect of human enterprise. There is nothing wrong with creating, acquiring, and applying knowledge. That is how humanity has advanced and evolved. However, it becomes a dangerous problem if we become attached to our answers and begin to relate to them as if they are "the truth". That relationship with knowledge limits our thinking and closes us off from other solutions and courses of action.

Consider that it is almost impossible to think about the future, a goal, or a problem without wanting or needing to know *how* to do something or *why* a given situation is the way it is. Both of these questions call for a response grounded in prior experience, belief, or knowledge.

It is difficult for most of us to contemplate that, in a real-time world, whatever answers we have to these questions of *how* and *why* are often irrelevant, obsolete, or wrong simply because complexity and the rate of change are both accelerating faster than our ability to analyze a situation and take action. When the world in general or a competitor in particular is changing faster than our capacity to implement change, our investments in understanding why something happens and in devising new ways of responding based on prior knowledge and experience may not pay off.

For example, after a handful of terrorists destroyed the World Trade Center in New York in September of 2001, the United States and nations around the world began to "close the gate after the fact" to prevent such occurrences from happening in the future. No one really knows how much effect massive global investments in security have had on stopping terrorism. It is a moot point: terrorists keep changing their tactics. Meanwhile, the general population becomes more and more captive to the solutions we've implemented in reaction to prior attacks and strategies. Our solutions often become new problems.

I am not suggesting all knowledge is irrelevant. But as we approach the future and try to deal with many of the concerns that we're facing in the world today, our relationship with knowledge shifts.

Knowledge is no longer our central concern. Rather, our central concern is taking care of what is needed and wanted in the moment.

Commit, Act, Learn

Common sense about learning is that we need to know something before we can commit and do something. Learning is, therefore, the prerequisite of commitment and action.

Traditionally when we encounter a new challenge or enter a new domain, the first question we typically ask is, "How?" While there is a place for "how" questions as a central concern and prerequisite for action, they can blind us to questions of "Who?", "When?", "What?" and "Where?".

We then face a dilemma. A "how" question is only answerable within some historical context or prior experience—and we have neither when we're in brand new situations facing brand new challenges.

When we make gaining or possessing knowledge a prerequisite for our willingness to commit, it traps us in a historically determined relationship with the future. That is, we can't have knowledge about something that hasn't happened or that doesn't exist—yet. Therefore, we cannot *commit* until we *know*.

In a real-time world, we are always committed, always in action, and always learning. Commitment, action, and learning are no longer separate or mutually exclusive activities. In a real-time world, commitment becomes the central organizing principle for navigating. It is the partner of action and learning. Expressing and coordinating our commitments, observing and declaring breakdowns are competencies that help us forward the action.

Admittedly, some people still approach learning for the sake of learning. However, for most, learning is relevant and useful only in the context of some intention or purpose. That intention or purpose gives us an organizing framework within which to interpret and "make sense" of the world. Most of us want to learn so that we can accomplish something, coordinate with others in some area, belong to a group, or participate in a particular conversation. Most of us want to learn because of a commitment we have or a commitment we intend to make.

Learning will give us the ability to fulfill that commitment, to make decisions and take actions informed by our new "sense-ability" to what we are observing relative to where we want to go.

Just In Time

Generalized knowledge on a subject may or may not be useful in real time. Specific knowledge, on the other hand, such as where to locate key ideas and sources of authority, will be absolutely necessary.

We might think of appropriation as the art of accessing the specific knowledge we need when we need it. We don't want to waste time tapping into the ever-growing mountains of knowledge for no reason. We learn just what we need to learn just in time. And we learn for the sake of something—to orient ourselves, to take care of a concern, or to successfully navigate uncharted territory in a "new world" as it arises. For example, I might read up on leadership and have a lot of general knowledge on the subject. But it will have little value beyond satisfying my curiosity unless and until I am in a situation which requires me to lead.

Early in my career, I found myself, without a background in management, accounting, consulting or business, working for a big accounting firm. I committed to becoming a partner and began a multi-year process of appropriating what I needed to perform, satisfy clients, and lead in a wide variety of situations. This facilitated my quickly becoming "maze bright" and soon one of the youngest partners in the history of the firm. I gathered whatever knowledge was still relevant and stable, as well as observations about relationships and anomalies. I brought together a variety of information sources, reading, listening, and watching what was going on inside and outside the firm to discern the most important players, their intentions, and the latest controversies. I focused on developing the capability to quickly grasp situation and context, learn a client's language and terminology, analyze problems as a team, create alignment on final rec-ommendations, and articulate and express conclusions in ways that could be understood and accepted by others.

I applied critical thinking to questions like:

- What's happening?
- What are our commitments?
- What is our role in the world?
- Where are we now?
- What are key relationships?
- What is the conventional wisdom?
- What are people's moods?
- What are the criteria for success?
- When will we act?

All this helped me observe what was present and what was missing. From there, I could start connecting the dots to see how we could innovate our way forward.

Relational Reality

We live in a relational reality.

As we have been saying throughout the book, we can see that we are our relationships. Probably the most important one we have is our relationship with the future. And that is generally in the background of all the different situations we find ourselves in during our lives. For example, when we create a vision, we are creating a relationship with the future as possibility. Therefore, we can be appropriating what we need to appropriate in order to manifest that vision. This is distinct from living into a future that we have predicted, in which we will be attempting to learn and apply whatever our historical practices and conversations proscribe as necessary to succeed, given the prediction.

To appropriate is to learn while living with the questions "Why not...?" and "What if...?" It is seeing relationships between fields of study that others may or may not have seen yet. Appropriating is a way of selecting from whatever we have access to in the moment and adapting what appears to be the best to the situation at hand.

Appropriation *across disciplines* is the opposite of specialization. Unlike multi-disciplinary approaches which often fail to successfully integrate information and knowledge or provide clarity for action, appropriation brings together ideas from across boundaries for a specific purpose by:

1. Looking at the fundamental principles of a particular "tree" of knowledge, identifying the trunk and the big branches, and then diving into where the individual leaves—ideas—hang

2. Deconstructing fundamental principles and comparing them with those in multiple other fields, and

3. Inventing different configurations of principles from various fields for emerging or new situations.

Appropriating across disciplines is one way in which game-changing entrepreneurs learn, adapt, and invent the future in real time.

This style of learning also allows us to not be limited by conventional knowledge. It encourages us to be more responsible, more focused, more discerning. More deliberate, more open, and more collaborative. We can be grounded realists, learning together, as we continue to relate to the future as a possibility.

We can appropriate a **sensibility to context**, the ability to be more aware of the various interpretations that all stakeholders bring to the conversations we are in. Not to make some interpretations "right" and others "wrong", but to actually get past the interpretations and listen for people's commitments and concerns. For their concerns reveal what they *truly* care about.

We can appropriate **curiosity and caring**, the head and the heart, both of which are imperative for our collective survival. Curiosity, as in bringing a sense of wonder, adventure, and discovery to our work. Caring, as in taking responsibility in every situation for ourselves, for each other, for our relationships, and for our planet.

Contextual Sensibility

Traditional learning focuses on content: the details of how something works, what has happened historically, the attributes of a particular product or service. However, we can no longer rely on knowledge being permanently valid. We are engaged in continuously disclosing new knowledge and expanding the boundaries of what is known.

Many thinkers now view knowledge as a continuing search for better interpretations. Contexts are the interpretations in which we are living, the historical and mental constructs (or worldviews) inside of which we think. These constructs represent the world surrounding us and the relationships we see between component parts. We are always navigating within a mosaic of these constructs and some interpretation of the world.

In the past, we could simply inherit whatever interpretation we were born into and then, based on trial and error, customize it in unique ways to make it our own. However, a worldview is not a finite set of "correct" propositions. Things move so fast in real time that we no longer have the luxury of being able to learn by trial and error inside of an inherited interpretation. Nowadays we need to be constantly aware of and responsible for how we observe the world.

In a real-time world, we regularly find ourselves in unfamiliar situations where we are either ignorant or simply out of touch with what's going on. While there will always be a lot more we can learn, we don't need comprehensive knowledge or deep understanding to be present and participating in life in a conscious and committed way. We can trust our commitments and our capability to appropriate whatever we need to deal with whatever is emerging.

We can begin an open-ended process of observing the world without our traditional biases and prejudices. We can observe and challenge our interpretations, reaffirm them, revise them, let go of old ones, appropriate and/or develop new ones as we go. We can choose which interpretation will best serve the future we want to create and commit to that as our context.

Contextual learning, therefore, is about developing a sensitivity to the context in which something happens and an awareness of the key *relationships* and *distinctions* in a particular domain of concern. In any situation, we can be attentive to the essentials. Who are the leaders? What are the fundamental principles governing what is happening? The values at play? The unique elements in the narratives of those involved? The key distinctions of their language(s)? Exposure to these enables us to become a different observer, a different listener. This kind of learning doesn't necessarily make us masterful experts in the field, but it creates an opening for engagement and the contribution of a grounded point of view.

Contextual learning happens much faster than traditional learning: it is a way of grasping these essentials. It is appropriation at its best.

Once we embody a particular interpretation, it will use us. "Use us" in the sense that when we master driving a car, our actions naturally correlate with what's needed and wanted in every moment. Once we embody a particular context, we can navigate and move in the world without having to analyze and think about every move.

Curiosity

Certainty is the enemy of learning. Certainty tells us what we know. And it gives us more of what we already have.

Certainty can kill curiosity.

Curiosity is learning's ally. Curiosity can not only reveal what we don't know, but it can also reveal our blindness to what we don't know we don't know. Curiosity connects us with who and what we care about. Curiosity jumpstarts a journey of discovery. Learning happens along the way.

As navigators, we are curious to observe what mood our colleagues and friends are in so we can help them better navigate the present. As entrepreneurs, we are curious to understand what people's concerns are so we can create something to take care of them. As global citizens, we are curious to explore what's possible in the future—without being naïve about what's occurring in the world in the present.

Curiosity is a foundational mood for innovation. A person in a curious mood brings a sense of wonder and openness to whatever they are considering, whether that is something specific or general. For instance, we can be specifically interested in how our particular mobile device works. Or we can be intrigued by the possibilities that smartphones give us generally.

Learning Together

Traditional education has focused on facilitating learning for individuals. Specifically, facilitating the acquisition of knowledge and skills. But both knowledge and skills become quickly outdated in a real-time world. And artificial intelligence can now acquire the knowledge and skills of many generations of individuals all at once.

Learning today is all about appropriating and sharing data and knowledge with more human beings so we can collectively see and dance with the relationships between things faster than we've ever done before. This is the essence of collaboration.

We are usually appropriating *for the sake of something*. We could all be appropriating for the sake of inventing the future. That appropriation is not necessarily an individual activity. Just as creating can happen faster when we are collectively collaborating on what we create (that is, co-creating), learning can happen faster when we are collectively learning together. Thomas Edison and his team in Menlo Park showed us back in the late 1800s that it is possible to co-learn and co-create together: their invention of the light bulb, the two-way telegraph, sound recording, motion pictures, and power utilities made today's telecommunications possible.

This co-learning is what is happening now when we open source the development of operating systems like Linux, publicly fund research that uses genome-editing technologies like CRISPR, and form non-profit research companies like OpenAI to create a safe path forward in the use of artificial intelligence. Co-learning is what is happening in those self-organizing, cross-functional teams in a company that somehow just keeps innovating better products. Co-learning is what is happening when we assign different sections of a potentially game-changing research project to different people scattered around the globe and have them all regularly bring back what they discover in their experiments to the whole collective. As we integrate our myriad inputs, learn what doesn't work well, and keep building on what does, we co-create our future.

Chapter 7

CARING:
the art of love

Caring is an expression of love, the antidote for
nihilism, and the possibility of expressing the very
best of who we are and who we can be
as human beings.

Why Love?

While the *homo sapiens* species evolves slowly and has changed very little over the millennia, who we are as human beings has and does change as our environment, our civilizations, and our practices change. In every age of human history, one or two central concerns have distinguished what it means to be a human being and tended to organize our relationship to reality and to life itself.

For the better part of human history, for example, our central concern was survival and, in this, there was very little difference between us and the rest of the animal kingdom. As our capacity for language developed and as human families and tribes grew into communities and towns, our concerns shifted toward commerce and cooperative enterprise. As religion became the dominant social institution during the Middle Ages in Europe, the prevailing concern of most people became personal salvation. The Renaissance put man at the center of all things and refocused society's priorities, interests, and organizing conversations on the pursuit of beauty, learning, and self-awareness.

In 1543, Copernicus published his heliocentric model of our universe, putting the Sun at its center and launching the Scientific Revolution. The focus of our concerns shifted yet again—this time to the pursuit of knowledge and control over a world of objects, of which human beings were understood to be just another kind of object. To this day, the concern for control pervades virtually every aspect of our social institutions, personal practices, common sense, and beliefs about what is necessary to cope with and succeed in life.

Our real-time world is disrupting this prevailing worldview. And in doing so it is once again disrupting who we understand ourselves to be.

We are realizing that, while we can have control over many physical processes, we do not and cannot have control over human experience, human expression, or human commitment. We essentially have no control over how reality occurs for us.

We do have a choice, however, in how we relate to what is occurring. In that choice lies the possibility of intentionally creating the future.

At the beginning of this book, I suggested no one has any idea what the future will be. Individuals continue to sketch out scenarios and make predictions: others continue to agree or disagree. But history will tell the story of what happened. And if recent history is any indicator, most of the predictions and scenarios will be wrong. My crystal ball is no better than anyone else's. But I think we can all agree that whatever *does* happen in the future is beyond our capacity to comprehend at this moment.

While we cannot predict what will happen, with or without awareness, we *can* and, like it or not, we *are* co-creating the future at every moment. This raises a question.

What are the central organizing principles for facilitating a world that can work for everyone?

Care and relationship.

In a real-time world, everything is relational. When we choose care as the context for our relating, we choose the possibility of being inclusive as we co-create a world that works.

While we don't know who we are becoming for sure, I expect we are becoming human beings who care about the moods and the quality of life of the people around us. Human beings who care about our relationships. Who care about our planet. Who care about our future.

I believe we are becoming caretakers.

The Prism

Most people will, at some point in their lives, engage in conversations about why they care or need care, why they love or don't love themselves or others. The problem with breaking down our experience of care and love into component parts, conceptualizing about causes, and attempting to apply conclusions to these areas of our life is singular: such reductionist thinking does not happen in real time. Care and love, on the other hand, are experienced "whole" in an instant. Analysis gives us, at best, only some insight into parts of that experience.

For many years, I considered relationship, communication, and love as three separate subjects. Communication was conversation. A relationship was like a "bowl" or the arena inside of which we conversed. Love was a quality experienced in a few very special relationships. That made sense.

But in a real-time world, reverting to common sense on these subjects doesn't always work. Our commonsense understanding of communication is that it is about information and understanding. Yet, we typically add our own meaning or prior interpretations, beliefs, and prejudices onto what is being communicated. Likewise, most of us think of love as a feeling, a product of the qualities we assess in ourselves or someone else, or as something that happens *to* us. Yet, this doesn't take into account that the quality of our relationship affects how we listen to each other—and how we listen can influence our understanding and our experience of love.

I now consider these three aspects of life—relationship, communication, and love—to be different dimensions of a single and indivisible whole, different facets of a prism that reflects who one is. In a real-time world, I suggest the name of the prism is care.

Caring is relating with others, in a space of love and communication, while acknowledging personal responsibility for all of our relationships. Rediscovering our capability for caring is essential to moving rapidly and powerfully, both as individuals and as communities, as we navigate emerging reality.

Care as Concern

Human beings care.

It is in our nature to do so.

To care is to be concerned. Specifically, to be concerned about alleviating suffering.

We care about people and things as a survival strategy. In doing so, we attach importance to life and to protecting ourselves, our families, our communities, and our institutions from harm.

We are taught who and what to focus our care on, and who and what not to focus on. Unfortunately, the emphasis is on what we care about, rather than on our innate capability to care in the first place.

In caring about people, we can express empathy and compassion.

In caring about abstractions like beauty and health, democracy and legacy, we reveal our values and priorities.

In caring, we can express who we are and to what we are committed.

Care as Context

Our conventional relationship to care focuses on the object of our care rather than the practice of caring. This has us easily confuse care and caring with the idea of "taking care of" or helping someone or something.

I propose, instead, that care is a context for relating to everything and everyone.

In a recent rebroadcast of a 2014 interview on National Public Radio, "Thom" raved about his company's founder and leader, a young man who repeatedly told his employees before he died of cancer to "Take care of your job, take care of yourself and take care of each other."[1] His words had inspired all the employees to choose a context of "care" as their ground of being in the world—even after his death.

That context did not prescribe what actions they should take. It left them free. They could care and, in a particular situation, choose to do something or choose to do nothing. Their behaviors and actions—or inaction—did not determine whether they cared or not. There is no "should" in care. They cared as an expression of responsibility, and so everything they did was an expression of their caring. In this way, care is like love.

I believe that care is an expression of love.

When I love, I am the context of the relationship with whomever or whatever I love. This alters my experience. It allows me to see possibilities I couldn't before and gives me choices I did not have in the absence of love. In the same way that a parent relates to their child, when "I love" is my ground of being, my context, and where I come from, then everything I do or say can be an expression of that love and care.

Care as a Way of Being

Our way of being in the world is mostly habit.

What may begin as a conscious behavior, an attitude, or a way of looking at things will, in time, become embodied and natural. For instance, in the caring professions, when we first learn to deliver primary care to a patient, we consciously make every move. Everything is distinct. Eventually, our actions, like any recurring experience, become transparent. In time, most of us stop being consciously aware of the intricate details of every particular procedure and automatically interact with the situation as appropriate.

This natural, inevitable shift towards transparency is both useful and dangerous. Useful because once we embody a new skill or habit, we no longer need to think about it. Dangerous because once we lose awareness of anything, we put ourselves at risk. We can easily fall into a pattern of taking things for granted that blind us to what is actually happening or could possibly happen. For all intents and purposes, we become like fish in a pond—cognitively blind—unable to see the water in which we are swimming.

This is why professional airline pilots and medical personnel use checklists and buddy systems to ensure that they perform *all* procedures and safety precautions in the correct order. Without these conscious checks, we are at risk of thinking something has been done when, in fact, it has not. Right after US Airways flight 1549 hit a flock of Canada geese and lost all engines on January 15th 2009, first officer Jeffrey Skiles ran through the checklist for engine restart. Meanwhile pilot Chesley B. "Sully" Sullenberger, on the other hand, relied on his competency, not a checklist, to dance with what was happening. He communicated clearly and succinctly with air traffic controllers, the passengers, and the crew while safely landing the plane in the Hudson River.

I often say that if you take a fish out of water, they instantly recognize the paradigm or medium in which they've been living. In much the same way, when something unexpected or unusual occurs to us, we can become aware of our cognitive blindness and have "instant paradigm recognition". For instance, imagine you're an American in Japan, where the small streets are seemingly littered with unlocked bicycles. Pick up one and get caught riding it without the correct papers and, in that moment, you will recognize how your way of being has been shaped by your culture. In Japanese culture, these bikes are not free for anyone to use: each one is licensed to a particular owner.

When I speak of care as a context and a way of being, I mean it is an orientation to the world. It organizes and shapes how we observe. A person who cares will observe myriad opportunities for caring and for expressing care. A person who does not care will rarely notice what is needed and wanted in a given situation or will be blind to all the opportunities that the caring person sees as obvious.

Our commonsense notion is that the world is filled with many people who care and many who do not. The prevailing belief is that whether a person cares or not is a function of their individual predispositions or character. While we will generally value someone who cares and appreciate gestures of caring, we don't generally see care and caring as a cultural phenomenon or as an innate capability. Neither do we typically consider that we can cultivate our capability to care and that the more we practice caring, the more important and central it can become to how we navigate in the world.

In a real-time world, it is more useful to view everyone as caring about something. When we think that someone doesn't care, we are actually saying that they don't care about what we care about and that they care about something different. We may or may not know what that is. This opens an opportunity for dialogue and mutual understanding of our differences and can also generate a basis for inventing new practices to take care of each other's concerns and what we care about.

We can learn to cultivate care as our way of being. Just as the potential for a garden exists in the seeds a gardener plants in the soil, the potential for this possible way of being exists within us. There will always be an element of contingency involved in life: a freak storm can wipe out the garden or an accident can disable our ability to focus our attention. However, for the most part, outcomes will primarily be a function of our commitment and consciousness around care.

In a real-time world, everyone is a gardener and everyone is a navigator. As navigators, we care where we are and where we've come from. And as gardeners, we care for the future as possibility by attending with care to moods, relationships, and what is happening in each moment.

Care as a Remedy

In 1982, Anne Herbert challenged a generation to practice "random kindness and senseless acts of beauty" as a counterpoint to "random acts of violence and senseless acts of cruelty". She was calling for a world in which each individual could participate in creating a culture (that is, an individual and collective way of being) in which kindness was a natural expression of being alive. She believed that, when a critical mass of the population embodied the practices of kindness and beauty, kindness and beauty would become foundational aspects of society, aspects as basic and omnipresent as the practices of wearing clothing or following traffic laws are in the developed world today.

This offers us yet another way of thinking about care and caring—as a remedy for egocentric and self-serving ways of being.

I've highlighted that, in a real-time world, we lack control and that our primary choice is in how we relate to everyone and everything. I've suggested that our commitments can provide us with direction and clarity about outcomes we intend to generate, but that the fulfillment of each commitment requires coordination and collaboration with others. In this sense, **care as a way of being** and **caring as a set of practices that express our care** are both essential to participating and working with others to co-create a shared future.

Caring as Commitment in Action

Caring is a rigorous commitment to the idea that everything we do or say has an impact. Caring is the intention to "do no harm" and to have a positive impact at every moment and in every situation. If the capacity to care is already central to being human, then we can cultivate this aspect of who we are in everything we do. We can bring care to everything from the mundane to the extraordinary, from crossing the street (because there is a very real possibility of being hit by a vehicle if we don't) to providing humanitarian aid in a famine (because it is possible that many will die from starvation if we don't).

For example, the practice of listening "for" possibility or "for" relationship is actually an expression of care. If we didn't care, we wouldn't listen to anyone—and we definitely wouldn't listen for either of these things. Being responsible for our circumstances, our relationships with others, and the situations we find ourselves in presumes caring. Making commitments and taking actions that are outside our comfort zone require the kind of exceptional motivation and courage that come with caring.

I am not suggesting caring as a way of avoiding anything negative by focusing solely on the positive. In fact, caring implies suffering. If there were no negative aspects to reality, there would be no reason and no need to care. It is *because* we human beings suffer, it is *because* many factors can threaten us, it is *because* many forces can harm us that we choose to care and commit to caring in action.

Caring is neither inherently sentimental nor "soft". It can be the tough love that sometimes involves punishment or restraints, such as when we give a child a curfew or a time-out. However, this doesn't mean that the results of our caring will always be what was intended. Generosity can be repaid with resentment and envy, even when no quid pro quo is expected or intended. Nor does our caring relieve us of any responsibility for the outcomes of our actions. Should something unintended occur, caring would have us take further actions, make corrections, and repair the damage to whatever extent that is possible.

Caring, therefore, includes learning from mistakes. It calls us to be willingly open and honest and invites us to celebrate the human spirit and the mysterious wonder of being alive.

How Caring is Expressed

I have suggested that everyone cares about something. Even when we say someone doesn't care, we are generally saying they don't care about something we care about.

Just as there are no "shoulds" about who and what we care about, there are no rules about what caring has to look like.

What we care about is reflected in what we pay attention to and how we spend the time we have. Likewise, our caring is reflected in our interests. I cannot pay attention to everything and everyone. I cannot do everything and be with everyone. And even though I may not be interested in everything and everyone, I can respect and value others' caring and interests.

A priority is a commitment that one thing is more important than something else and usually correlates with where we spend our time. Perhaps, in this way, priorities are the most telling indicator of our care. But they are not a limitation on our caring. We can be caring even when we're asked to do something we're not interested in by shifting how things occur for us so that our care comes into play again. For example, I may not have the slightest interest in a tour of my friend's office building. Not caring would be a reflection of my insensitivity to how important this is to them, how proud they are of its technological achievements, and my blindness to how important this environment is to their well-being. If I care about our relationship and I'm paying attention, I'll notice all this and might make time for the tour or apologize for not having time and acknowledge them for what they've built.

These expressions of our care and our practices for caring are never right or wrong. Neither are they good or bad. They simply reflect an orientation to the world and a certain level of consciousness about our relationships and our interrelatedness.

None of this is new. In many traditions, the golden rule to do unto others as we would have them do unto us is one of the oldest prescriptions for living together. Unfortunately, like most maxims, it is easy to agree with, but less helpful when trapped in counter-productive or historical patterns. One might say not to worry, but that maxim doesn't help when you are worried.

Rather than focus on the differences between our individual "care", I propose that we focus on the practices of caring and on consciously creating care as a context for living.

For example, when my way of being is care, I can listen attentively to what you care about and I can also be interested in other interests you may have.

Again, what this looks like for different people in different situations will vary. When I listen to a friend share a problem they're dealing with, the conversation is often quite direct and may easily finish in 10 minutes. When someone else listens to one of their friends in a similar way, the conversation may be quite indirect and could easily take an hour. We listen differently, but caring is a way of being for both of us. Our caring is not a function of time.

Which brings us to an interesting observation. It takes no time to care. Just as it takes no time to love.

This runs contrary to the popular idea that equates the context of care and love with activities associated with both. This can have us believing that we can't love or care for everybody, because then we would have no time for ourselves.

But when we hold care and love as our way of being, we can bring this context with us as we move rapidly from one conversation to another. Every moment and every conversation can be an opportunity for expressing care. An opportunity for expressing who we are.

Cultivating Caring

Learning to care is mostly learning to observe and preparing ourselves to respond in each moment as a matter of choice.

Cultivating caring begins with changing how we listen and relate. Each of us can make a decision to shift how we relate to our circumstances, others, and even ourselves. We can start to listen and relate with compassion to ourselves and others. We can engage with challenges and life coming from a context of love, empathy, and appreciation. Doing this requires some discipline for a short period until the compassionate way of relating becomes a habit. Mindfulness techniques and practices can help us become self-aware, better observers of our selves and others and the details in a situation. We can cultivate "triggers" to remind us to stop, breathe, and notice—and to then choose, rather than react.

So what can we do when we think we *should* care, but honestly don't?

I propose this is normally more a reflection of our mood than a choice not to care. In other words, caring or not caring is not a decision we typically make. Some things appear to us in a way that pulls for our caring and others may not.

Care is a function of how we observe, and how we observe is a function of our way of being and where we're coming from. If we are coming from a context of fear, then everything is a threat. If we are coming from a context of anger, then everything is an inflammatory aggravation. If we are coming from a context of care, then everything is an opportunity to express our care.

Love & Care

The source of our capacity for love and relationship—as well our ability to care—is, at best, a theory and, for most of us, a mystery.

Some talk of love as a feeling, an emotion, or a thing. Some believe it is dependent on circumstances, defined by specific behaviors, or persistent and unshakeable.

I believe love is a choice. A choice in how we relate to ourselves and everyone and everything in our lives. We can choose to love anyone and anything we care about.

I think of love as a gift. Love is granting ourselves or another the space, the freedom, and the choice to be the way we are, as well as any other way we choose to be. Love is granting people the freedom to choose.

In other words, love is a commitment that people are whole and sufficient the way they are: they do not need to be fixed, controlled, or manipulated into feeling or believing anything other than what they do. As a commitment, love needs to be continually re-created in every moment in every relationship. In other words, love is a space and, as such, doesn't persist in time.

From this perspective, any other basis for relating is not a relationship with another human being. Any other basis for relating is a projection of your point of view about yourself or them—not a relationship between human beings. In other words, you are relating to your own point of view and assessments or to the other person as an object and, therefore, relating to them as part of the circumstances of life.

I don't think care is the same as love, but I don't believe we can care without love, just as I think it is impossible to love without care.

Without a background context of love, I don't believe we can respect and work with those with whom we disagree, those who may have severe problems, or those we don't like and whom we perhaps even consider to be our enemy. In a real-time world, love, like care, is a practical necessity for survival, not just an indulgence in the "love thy neighbor as thyself" ethic. Any historically rooted notions that divide us and generate resistance will leave us reacting to anyone whom we cannot love and, therefore, disconnect us from our rapidly changing landscape and whatever possibilities are emerging. This also limits our capacity to trust one another or ourselves, to learn from each other, to collaborate and coordinate our actions.

In 1958, Dr. Martin Luther King, Jr. wrote of the connective nature of what the Greeks called *agape*, the unconditional love that serves regardless of circumstances:

"Another basic point about agape is that it springs from the need of the other person—his need for belonging to the best in the human family.... Agape is not a weak, passive love. It is love in action.... Agape is a willingness to go to any length to restore community.... It is a willingness to forgive, not seven times, but seventy times seven to restore community.... If I respond to hate with a reciprocal hate I do nothing but intensify the cleavage in broken community. I can only close the gap in broken community by meeting hate with love." [2]

In this sense, agape is the foundation for a world of care in which we are sensitive to other's concerns and in which our choices reflect our commitment to our individual and collective well-being.

Perhaps agape is the most powerful and compelling driver of action. As Dr. Eben Alexander, the neurosurgeon who published a best-selling book about his own near-death experience, believes, it is simply the basis of everything.

"Love is, without doubt, the basis of everything. Not some abstract, hard to fathom kind of love, but the day-to-day kind that everyone knows—the kind of love we feel when we look at our spouse and our children, or even our animals. In its purest and most powerful form, this love is not jealous or selfish, but unconditional. This is the reality of realities, the incomprehensibly glorious truth of truths that lives and breathes at the core of everything that exists or that ever will exist.... Not much of a scientific insight? Well, I beg to differ. I'm back from that place, and nothing could convince me that this is not only the single most important emotional truth in the universe, but also the single most important scientific truth as well."[3]

POSTSCRIPT

We are living history every minute of every day. And we are living at a moment in history when our entire worldview is morphing from one reality to another. This global phenomenon is transforming our relationship with everything. Every institution and every area of life is being affected. Only time is real and constant in any scenario of the future.

This kind of meta-change is not the first paradigm shift that humanity has experienced. It is, however, unprecedented, primarily due to the speed of technological progress and the fact that our common sense about the relationship between the past and the future is breaking down. In the 1980s corporate video "The Business of Paradigms", Joel Barker proclaimed that paradigm shifts challenge all of our assumptions about everything such that everyone and everything (re)starts at zero. Nothing can be taken for granted. We are literally living in a new world. We are—all of us—beginners again.

The premise of this book has been that we are living in a real-time world in which the gap between the past and the future is disappearing. The gap is "now", a present in which we can see how rapidly the "past" is changing and how rapidly we are creating many possible futures. We are living in a world of such complexity that knowledge alone—often obsolete even before we learn it—is no longer the core requirement for success. A world in which we lack control over almost everything and in which we can no longer rely on our predictions and forecasts to inform our commitments and plans.

I believe that the political and social discord and political polarization we've witnessed throughout the world since the beginning of this century are the inevitable and essential prelude to a widely experienced "awakening" to the fact that we cannot survive as a species until we learn to navigate change and life in real time. The core requirements for navigating? More awareness, more appropriation in the "now", more consciousness about the worldviews we hold, more caring, more clarity about the commitments we make to the future we want to co-create.

We don't know what this "new" world will look like. But we can surmise that it will be organized around a kind of epochal concern, a central value, or organizing principle. I believe that principle is care and caring.

First, we are already hard-wired to care. We have evolved as caring beings. We've always had communities of care and practices for caring within those communities.

Second, I believe the real-time nature of the world today is calling for a context that can include everyone while, at the same time, empower diversity. Technology is enabling us to both recognize and participate at higher and higher levels of inclusion, while at the same time allowing us maximum freedom and independence. Third, we are entering the age of the "quantum" self, an age in which we are both individuals and also an indivisible hologram of the whole community. And last, but not least, care as a central organizing principle allows for us to acknowledge and deal with each other and all of the situations of day-to-day living in a context of compassion. It allows for both the wonder and the mystery. It allows for both the discomfort of living with permanent uncertainty and the exhilaration and aliveness of being present to the challenges and the satisfaction of creating a world that works for all of us.

I propose that, as we enter this new world, there are two main questions we as individuals, as a community, and as a civilization will now want to concern ourselves with:

1. Who are we choosing to become in the face of all these changes?

2. What capabilities can we cultivate to sustain our conscious evolution and create a world that can work for everyone?

While we can't know the future, I am suggesting that we can prepare ourselves and our children to be responsible for whatever happens and to benefit from all the breakdowns, anomalies, surprises, and disconnects associated with meta-change. Even as our narrative of who we are and what life is and how the world works changes, we still have choice. We can become self-absorbed spectators trying to predict the future and indulging in endless conversations about change, what we like or don't like, and whether we agree or disagree with what is happening. Or we can observe moods in ourselves, in others, and in our communities; explore new practices; commit to new learning; and participate in conversations that create the future. We can become participants in the flow of life, cultivating these skills of anticipation and making prudent moves as we navigate change.

Our daily conversations reveal whether we are spectators witnessing what's happening or participants actively creating our relationships with everyone and everything in our lives.

By no means do I claim that the conversational capabilities discussed in this book are sufficient to what we may face in the future. Emerging realities are unknowable. The possibility we are as human beings is unknown. Just as the ability to speak and to write were dormant in human beings for ages, we may soon discover other capabilities we've never known we possess that will open up a whole new dimension to life. Advances in science, neuroscience, and philosophy are transforming our understanding of human beings as autonomous objects and independent psychological entities. We now understand the linguistic nature of being itself. Many people are even experiencing a breakthrough in the narrative of what it is to be a human being.

The key in all this will be to keep cultivating our innate capabilities—and to explore others as they appear as well— while we navigate whatever new worlds are emerging.

NOTES

Preface

1. José Ortega y Gasset, *Mission of the University,* edited & translated by Howard Lee Nostrand (New York, NY: W.W. Norton & Company, 1974), p. 73.

Real Time

1. Peter Diamandis, "Why UBI Works", *Huffington Post,* May 8, 2017. Accessed March 5, 2018 at https://www.huffingtonpost.com/entry/why-ubi-works_us_590fee1ae4b0f71180072461d.

2. Eckhart Tolle, *The Power of Now: A Guide to Spiritual Enlightenment* (Novato, CA and Vancouver, Canada: New World Library and Namaste Publishing, 1999).

3. This saying, or variants of it, has been variously attributed to Josh Billings (1874), Artemius Ward (1897), Mark Twain ((1899), Abraham Lincoln (1900) and Will Rogers (1978). Accessed January 7, 2018 at https://quoteinvestigator.com/2015/05/30/better-know/#note-11302-9.

Accepting

1. William Hutchison Murray, The Scottish Himalaya Expedition (London: Dent, 1951).

2. Anonymous" (Bill Wilson), *Alcoholics Anonymous: The Story of How Many Thousands of Men and Women Have Recovered from Alcoholism,* 16th edition (Hazelden, 1991).

3. The Serenity Prayer was originally attributed to American theologian Reinhold Niehbuhr in his sermons dating back as early as 1934. This version is the one popular in twelve-step programs. Accessed June 10, 2018 at https://en.m.wikipedia.org/wiki/Serenity_Prayer.

4. Brené Brown, *Daring Greatly: How the Courage to be Vulnerable Transforms the Way We Live, Love, Parent and Lead* (Gotham Books, 2012). Accessed June 10, 2018

at https://www.goodreads.com/author/quotes/
162578.Bren_Brown?page=3.

Being

1. René Descartes, *Discourse on the Method of Rightly Conducting One's Reason and of Seeking Truth in the Sciences,* Part IV (Leiden, Netherlands: 1637).

2. This quote is popularly attributed to Shaw. Another version of the quote ("...the self is not something one finds; it is something one creates.") has been attributed to Dr. Thomas Szasz in his book *The Second Sin* (Anchor Books, 1973), p. 49.

3. This idea that we are language is not new. See the work of philosophers J.L. Austin, John Searle, and Fernando Flores.

4. State of the Global Workplace Report: Executive Summary (Washington, DC: Gallup, 2017), p. 4.

Listening

1. Eckhart Tolle, *The Power of Now: A Guide to Spiritual Enlightenment* (Novato, CA and Vancouver, Canada: New World Library and Namaste Publishing, 1999).

2. Charles Eisenstein, *The More Beautiful World Our Hearts Know is Possible* (Berkeley, CA: North Atlantic Books, 2013).

3. Otto Whittaker Jr., "I am the Nation", *Norfolk and Western Railway Company Magazine*, January 15, 1976 front cover. Accessed January 21, 2018 at http://www.bartleby.com/73/65.html.

4. "I am India" song on YouTube. Accessed January 21, 2018 at https://www.youtube.com/watch?v=3_WFsCiLw6s.

5. Thich Nat Hanh, *Interbeing: Fourteen Guidelines for Engaged Buddhism* (Full Circle Publishing Ltd., 2003).

6. Gloria P Flores, *Learning to Learn and the Navigation of Moods: The Meta-Skill for the Acquisition of Skills* (2016), p. 23-24.

7. Adapted from Alan Sieler's "Eight Moods of Life", *Coaching to the Human Soul: Ontological Coaching and Deep Change*, Volume II (Blackburn, Victoria: Newfield Australia, 2007), p. 193.

Communicating

1. Fernando Flores best articulated this connection between relationship and communication in his 1979 doctoral dissertation "Management and Communication in the Office of the Future". In this foundational work, he distinguished several key ideas which have transformed how I think about relationship. First, what is always present is communication; second, relationship and communication are heads and tails of the same coin; third, relationships manifest in our conversations and moods; fourth, access to change is through communication; and fifth, we are always creating our reality in conversations.

2. Rex Harrison. *A Damned Serious Business* (New York, NY: Bantam Books, 1991), p. 242.

3. Ibid, p. 150.

4. Victor E. Frankl. Accessed June 22, 2018 at https://www.goodreads.com/author/quotes/2782.Viktor_E_Frankl?page=3.

5. Robert C. Solomon and Fernando Flores. *Building Trust in Business, Politics, Relationships and Life* (New York, NY: Oxford University Press, 2001), p. 13.

6. Václav Havel. "Forgetting We Are Not God". Speech given at Stanford University on September 29, 1994. Accessed February 4, 2018 at Institute on Religion and Public Life website at https://www.firstthings.com/article/1995/03/forgetting-we-are-not-god.

Appropriating

1. Peter M. Senge. *The Fifth Discipline: The Art and Practice of the Learning Organization* (New York, NY: Doubleday Business, 1990).

2. Mohamed Amin on Wikipedia. Accessed June 23, 2018 at https://en.m.wikipedia.org/wiki/Mohamed_Amin.

3. Hans Rosling, Ola Rosling, and Anna Rosling Rönnlund. *Factfulness: Ten Reasons We're Wrong About the World—And Why Things Are Better Than You Think* (New York, NY: Flatiron Books, 2018).

4. Kevin Maney. "Cyberspeak", *USA Today*, July 5, 2005. Accessed June 22, 2018 at https://usatoday30.usatoday.com/tech/columnist/kevinmaney/2005-07-05-famous-quotes_x.htm.

5. Robert Strohmeyer. "The 7 Worst Tech Predictions of All Time", ABC News, December 31, 2008. Accessed June 22, 2018 at https://abcnews.go.com/Technology/PCWorld/story?id=6558231 and Robert Metcalfe on Wikipedia at https://en.m.wikipedia.org/wiki/Robert_Metcalfe.

6. Jay Yarrow. "Here's What Steve Ballmer Thought about the iPhone Five Years Ago", *Business Insider,* referring to interview between Ballmer and David Lieberman, originally published in *USA Today*, 2007. Accessed June 22, 2018 at https://usatoday30.usatoday.com/money/companies/management/2007-04-29-ballmer-ceo-forum-usat_N.htm and at http://www.businessinsider.com/heres-what-steve-

ballmer-thought-about-the-iphone-five-years-ago-2012-6.

7. Fernando Flores. *Conversations for Action & Collected Essays: Instilling a Culture of Commitment in Our Working Relationships* (2012), Kindle edition, pp. 44-45.

Caring

1. Glynn Washington interview of "Thom" from San Francisco. "Creep", *Snap Judgment* on NPR, December 26, 2014. Accessed February 5, 2018 at https://www.npr.org/2014/12/26/373265993/creep.

2. Dr. Martin Luther King Jr., "An Experiment in Love", *A Testament of Hope: The Essential Writings and Speeches of Martin Luther King, Jr.* (New York, NY: HarperCollins, 1986), pp. 16-20.

3. Dr. Eben Alexander, *Proof of Heaven: A Neurosurgeon's Journey into the Afterlife* (New York, NY: Simon & Schuster, 2012), p. 71.

PROFILE

Jim Selman has worked for over 50 years as a change management consultant to major corporations. In the 1980s, he co-founded Transformational Technologies, an operating network of over 70 consulting organizations in the United States and Europe, and was the first to distinguish  coaching as an alternative to traditional control-oriented management. A committed student and teacher in the field of transformation, Jim has become a recognized thought leader in designing organizational cultures and teaching transformational leadership. His current company, Paracomm Partners International, has successfully led large-scale transformation initiatives for organizations in Europe, Russia, and the Americas.

Jim is also founder of The Eldering Institute, an organization committed to the proposition that aging can be a conversation for possibility rather than a story of inevitable decline and loss. He currently lives in southern California with his wife Darlene.

Made in the USA
San Bernardino, CA
19 March 2019